Collected
FAT

by Cap'n Fatty Goodlander

Dedication:

To my lovely daughter, Roma Orion, who is an
endless source of joy to me.

TABLE OF CONTENTS

Serious Tings

You Gotta Regatta

Afterword

Excerpts from previous books

Cap'n Fatty Goodlander

Introduction

Cap'n Fatty on the bow of *Wild Card*

I never wanted this book published; in fact, I fought long and hard against it. I felt that it had been risky enough foisting this pseudo-literary swill off on a brain-damaged editor *once*; surely redredging it would be pressing my luck.

Besides, why subject my readers to even more salt-stained abuse? What had *they* ever done to *me* to deserve more of my sun-crazed, venom-sprinkled writing?

However, my wife eventually wore down my resistance with a very clever argument. "We need the money, Fatty," she said. "We're broke.

Collected Fat

We've no food. Worse yet, *we've no rum!* Either release another book... or get an honest job... or sober up!"

Pretty persuasive, eh?

And, although I'm no longer totally enthralled with some of my earliest, most radical pieces of writing—many of my far-flung readers still feel that my *worst* efforts were my *best* writing.

I've always been astounded at the number of requests I get for reprints. "Send me a copy of that story where you puke on the nuns..." or "remember the story where you smashed a Baltic 51 into the reef off Antigua?" or "do you have a copy of the one where the West Indian fisherman screws the charter cook on the foredeck?"

Yes, indeed, I do.

Somehow, in the sweet innocence of my youth, I always thought that being a professional writer would be, well, sort of refined and dignified. The savage reality, at least for me, has been anything *but*.

I'll be strolling down a pristine beach in the Caribbean with my wife and child, and an obviously drunk, rum-addled, ganja-reeking derelict will suddenly lurch out from between the palm trees (as he zips himself up). "Hey, HEY!" he'll scream wildly as he stumbles toward us. "Hey Fatty... FATMAN!"

I'll have to stop, carefully position myself upwind of his odoriferous, battle-scarred body, and sign a dog-eared copy of one of my books.

"Are all bums your fans?" my daughter once asked me.

"No," I replied regretfully, "but all of my fans are bums!"

Another strange fact: hundreds of faithful readers have informed me that *Chasing the Horizon* is the only book they've '...read cover-to-cover since High School!'

"Great," my wife moaned. "You've written a best-seller for *people who don't buy books*—you're the favorite author of *illiterates*!"

So—there you have it, folks. Abject poverty compels me to, once again, throw myself on the mercy of my long-suffering readers.

These stories are among the best I've ever written.

Imagine how that makes me feel.

Mind the Rudder
Or Meet the Rock,

DIS AND DAT

Carolyn on *Wild Card* in the Virgin Islands

Cruising Wives

If a West Indian man goes into town to find a woman to marry, he is said to 'look a wife.' Single cruising sailors here in the Caribbean conduct similar spousal searches in every port they 'reach.' Of course, cruising sailors are searching for a specific type of seagoing woman to share their sailing lifestyle with.

"Get yourself a pear-shaped woman," advised one old salt. "They're broad of beam, and carry their weight low for extra stability. Stay away from blondes, chicks who like gold jewelry, or any babe who wears red nail polish. In addition, DSQ 'em if they have clean hair, wear make-up, or smell good. The more they resemble a sturdy cruising vessel, the better."

Sensible advice.

Of course, we're strictly talking about cruising wives here. Racing sailors chase after a totally different variety of woman.

They're after women with high-aspect rigs and plenty of top-hamper. If they have a good run aft and a cute little transom, so much the better.

But the last thing in the world a cruising sailor wants is a 'fast' wife.

Likewise, sportfishing wives are a totally different kettle of fish. They can be spotted by all the fillet knife cuts on their gnarled hands, and, alas, their pungent odor. They have a dangerous tendency to drink till they 'eel' over, totally kelpless. Sometimes while floundering around drunk they injure themselves so badly they require the medical services of a skilled sturgeon. When approached in an amorous manner, they often react negatively by slurring, "Not tonight, dear. I have a haddock!"

If the fisher-husband ignores this standard refusal, and continues to talk to his wife seductively she often becomes hard-of-herring. His insistence makes her crabby, while he thinks she's being shellfish with her sexual favors...

"A good cruising wife should be as strong as a donkey," agreed another long term Caribbean sea gypsy. "After all, most of the time ashore she'll be lugging around lots of heavy stuff in canvas bags. Why, once I walked right passed my wife in Philipsburg because I didn't recognize her ashore without her laundry bag, propane tank, block of ice, sack of groceries, and case of Heineken!"

"It's good if they're deaf and dumb, don't bruise easily, and are into some mild S&M," said a trendy young sailor stylishly wearing a pair of gold fishhook earrings and some stainless steel Nicro-Fico nipple clamps. "That way, when you tack—while yelling at them as you drop the winch handle on their toes while whipping them with the bitter end of the Kevlar jib, they can't complain too loudly."

"Shy away from women with addictive personalities," warned one jaded Caribbean cruiser who had obviously learned his lesson the hard way.

"My previous wife was addicted to water. She was an absolute *lush* when it came to water. She wanted to drink it, bathe in it, cook with it—even brush her teeth with it! She'd go on drinking binges; once I found her passed out under the drinking fountain at the Juliana airport. It was terrible—she hid bottles of *Perrier* all around the boat... and once I caught her in the bathroom at Chesterfields with a plastic straw over her shoulder into the toilet tank..."

A number of sailors felt sorry for the guy. One guy from Anguilla said, "Mon, you must've been happy to divorce she, to wash your hands of dat crazy bitch..."

"Didn't have to," interrupted the fellow. "She ran off with one of those NECOL boys, the one who fixes and maintains the marine desalinators. Of course, it's all water under the bridge now..."

"It isn't all just physical," agreed another sailor. "A lot has to do with attitude. A cruising wife should be frugal, yet flexible. When she's shopping for groceries at Sang's, Food Center or A Foo Extra, she should be squeezing those pennies so hard that Abraham Lincoln gets tears in his eyes. However, when she rows ashore at night to pay your bar tab at the *Green House*—well, there's no reason to be *too* miserly!"

"Once, I met the perfect cruising wife," said one fellow lustfully. "She flossed with manila docklines, ate only brown rice soaked in oily bilgewater, and happily dressed in Hefty trash bags when she dressed at all. She was allergic to soap, perfume, and clean underwear. She enjoyed grinding fiberglass; said she found the itchy feeling erotic. She was a work-a-holic who got high sniffing varnish fumes, and could bring a 45# CQR up on deck as easy as a yo-yo. She *liked* cockroaches, head odors, and mildew..."

"So what was the problem," someone asked.

"The problem was," said the sailor glumly, "that she had an IQ of 75, only 25 points below average..."

"Yep, same old story," said the old salt who had started the conversation. "She was far too smart to get mixed up with a bunch of old sea gypsies like us..."

Crewed Sex

I'd met Jon and Alison (names changed to protect the guilty) numerous times. They were one of the hardest working, most dedicated, friendliest, most personable chartering couples in the Lesser Antilles. He was a careful skipper, and she was a perfect hostess. Their boat, though hard-used in the fully-crewed chartering trade, was always kept absolutely immaculate.

They were also good business people. They were booked solid for the season, and we'd heard rumors that they'd recently been doing a lot of back-to-back charters.

"You gotta make it while you can," Jon had told me during our last rum-filled meeting at the Ad Inn.

However, as they sailed into the nearly deserted anchorage on the south side of Antigua, I almost didn't recognize them. She was at the helm, zooming into the harbor like a hyped-up throttle jockey with a nose full of crystal meth. He was on the foredeck in his little red *Speedo* swimming trunks, hopping around like a little kid who had to pee.

Their eyes looked crazed, dazed, and full of fire.

Their large ketch-rigged boat was moving fast, that's for sure. It was under both full sail and full power. Finally, Alison throttled back, and took the diesel out of gear. Then she leapt out of the amidship cockpit onto the starboard side deck, took out the barrette from her long, blond hair, and yelled with a sexy growl, "It's out of gear, BIG BOY!"

Jon was forward, messing with the anchors. His muscular chest was puffing in-and-out like a chameleon doing push-ups. He finally managed to splash a large CQR anchor from his massive bow-roller, and then ran aft—trotting rather ape-like, I thought.

At the mast, he cast off the jib halyard. The jib immediately rattled down, its now-forgotten clew half in the water off the port bow. Next, he cast off the main halyard.

Then he turned to her—just as he appeared to begin to seriously hyper-ventilate. "Come to Papa!" he bellowed hoarsely. "Come to Papa NOW!"

"YESSSSSSSSSSSSSSSS!" she screamed as she leapt toward him.

They came together in a frantic, chest-thumping, embrace amidships—just as the anchorline drew taut, the boat spun sharply on her heel, and main sail fluttered down over them like a giant Dacron prophylactic.

I could see them moving spasmodically under the sail; they looked like dogs wrestling. The loud, base sounds they were making were incredible: yelps, moans, groans, and grunts.

Then they slithered sweatily out from under the still flapping main sail, and were down the companionway in a blur of damp flesh.

Both parts of her two-piece bikini shot out from the main hatch, and his swim trunks came flying out through the aft cabin porthole.

For a moment, there was almost silence, but the still waters of the bay suddenly began to ripple outwards from their stout vessel... which had started to vibrate and hop up and down and jiggle and flex... and then the halyards started to slap/slap/slap on the aluminum mast like during Hurricane Hugo...

...all this motion and noise increased in pitch, tempo and intensity— until, Until, UNTIL... the boat seemed to literally explode. All of its hatches, ports, and ventilators were violently wrenched open, and smoke/steam poured from its twisted & torn bronze orifices...

...then there were two strangled yelps of utter animal release... one high pitched and the other rather low... and then a total, deep silence.

My own wife had rushed on the deck of our boat at the sound of the explosion. "Do you think their propane stove blew up," she asked with concern.

"No, dear," I said with a gentle, knowing smile, "I don't think this is, er... a 'bun-in-the-oven' type problem. I think they are just a typical charter couple, and this is their first day off alone in long, long time. They deserve a little audio..."

"Ah ha," said my wife, suddenly catching my drift. *"That's* why they call it a lay-day!"

Think about it. Most charter boats are run by adult couples. Most adult couples either engage in regular acts of procreation, or like to keep in practice.

This creates problems for chartering couples, obviously. Of course, being imaginative, innovative people—they've come up with a number of clever solutions.

"Loud generators," said one skipper. "The louder, the better. Don't get a smooth-running four cylinder generator. Instead, opt for an unbalanced two-lunger which vibrates so much that it is tough to keep it bolted down to its beds. *That's* the key to a happy charter-marriage."

There are other, less radical, solutions. The "strand them on the beach" ploy is a tried and true method. The "send them ashore in the outboard dinghy with only a cup of gas" is another common one. The "we dragged anchor and had to move" trick usually works.

Most charter couples use a combination of all of the above. Some carry windsurfers aboard solely to "lose a guest down wind" for an hour or so.

One lusty skipper was reported to have said to his mate—when their sole charter couple were both swept off the bowsprit by a huge wave... "They look like fairly strong swimmers to me. How much time do you think we've got?"

"My mother warned me," lamented one experienced-but-still-game charter wife. "But I thought she was warning me about *crude* sex, not crewed sex!"

Fatty and Carolyn on *Wild Card* in Tonga

Viva La Difference

I love cruising the French West Indies. It is truly a tropical paradise for the anchoring impaired. I willingly embrace all the unique aspects of the trans-cultural sailing experience: the floating plastic bags in the harbor, those urine scented palm tree trunks, the astounding arrogance of those purse-waving, limp-wristed, round-hatted government officials.

Where else but in Paris can you be treated so rudely, lied to so shamelessly, short-changed so quickly!

I particularly admire the cruising boats of the French West Indies—those slab-sided, rusty, multichined, engineless tin cans which continuously rattle along the Antilles from St. Barts to Guadeloupe to Martinique... often leaving in the dead of night...

Years ago, I thought that the shabby appearance of these crudely-welded boats was because of the abject poverty of their owners... but now I realized that it is more of a matter of cultural priorities. (Even the shabbiest of these boats often have six or seven almost new inflatable dinghies stowed out-of-sight belowdecks—so the owners can't be too destitute, eh?)

Some people complain that the French islands are too expensive. There is, alas, some truth to this. Buying a (tiny) cup of coffee and a pastry *sans* filling at a seaside bistro in Le Saintes costs about the same as... purchasing the entire island of Hispaniola.

But let's ignore those pricey restaurants for a moment: French countries *do* offer a number of opportunities to save money. Surely, a Caribbean sailor need not invest too much of his precious cruising kitty in soap, dentists, or barbers.

What more does a French sea gypsy need beyond a (stained) pair of cut-offs, a (stained) pillow sack of garlic, a (cheap) bottle of rot-gut rum, and a nice new dinghy (yours).

Of course, the French *yachtsmen* are different. They have trendy yachting caps, purple boatshoes, and gold dive watches (which are so heavy they require their own buoyancy compensators). Their sleek plastic go-fast boats are filled with every imaginable water toy—except for sail covers, fenders, or a basic *How To Sail* book.

French (ocean) racing sailors are well-known throughout the world. They have really left their mark(s) here in the Caribbean. (Ask any local Awlgrip specialist!) Even while asleep these sailing adventurers can keep their boats moving fast—and if they pull up their anchors after they've dragged out of the harbor, their boats will move even *faster!*

Of course, it isn't fair to single out only the French. Surely the Americans are far uglier 'world travelers' in most respects. These dollar-dominated yanks are famous for their provincial, narrowed-minded views. "The problem with British sailors is that they are all repressed homosexuals," said one right-wing, Euro-phobic American yachtsmen recently, "and the problem with the French is that they are not—repressed, that is."

(Boy George excepted, this view of British yachtsmen is widely held by Americans—yet almost totally erroneous. Americans, alas, often confuse cross-dressing and self-flagellation with being gay—so this wide-spread confusion is fairly understandable... if, alas, unfortunate.)

"This type of stereotypical cultural and sexual typecasting is ultimately beneath one's dignity," commented a Dutch sailor from Sint Maarten in response to all of the above. "Unless, of course, there is a way to make a *profit* on it..."

Certainly the most twisted group of modern sailors cruising the French West Indies are card-carrying, flag-waving members of the dreaded Seven Sleaze Cruising Association.

This is an international organization of cruising sailors who have pledged to continuously complain about the prices ashore, the quality of life in the harbor, and the entire banking industry of whatever unfortunate little country they happen to be wearing out their welcome in.

Their official motto is: "This island stinks, but it didn't 20 years ago when I first cruised through here... (*Lucky me!*).. but now everyone decent and honorable is dead... so I'm moving on..."

Many of the American members of the Seven Sleaze Cruising Association are retired military. This means they are living on fixed incomes and social security, and, thus, are so cheap they squeak. They are famous for squeezing their pennies so hard Abe Lincoln weeps.

Their favorite pastime is gathering in *someone else's* cockpit, sipping warm rum-and-plastic-tasting-water from chipped jelly jars... and discussing which country in the world has the cheapest toilet paper, denture adhesive, and prune juice.

They even publish a monthly newsletter which reports on which island nations currently have the most docile natives....

Needless to say, Seven Sleaze Cruising Association members normally don't stay too long in the French West Indies. It is considered too expensive... too many people having fun... too much laughter and good vibes... too much artful living.

They prefer a more dour and puritanical sea-going lifestyle.

"Look for a country with a large number of protected harbors and a high infant morality rate," advised a particularly stingy, grey-bearded Caribbean sea gypsy. "Living is usually pretty cheap there. Beware of countries with hospitals or schools or other governmental institutions which coddle the local populace..."

No, these massively miserly 'econo' cruising folk don't last too long in the FWI. They have almost polar-opposite attitudes from the free-spending, fun-loving French.

The average sailing Frenchman is a hedonist. He wants to enjoy every second of his life upon the sea—no matter how much damage he causes to the vessels around him.

Thus, the secret of cruising in the French West Indies is to not struggle against the prevailing Gallic attitude—in essence, to go with the cultural flow. Bump into a few boats as you tour the harbor. Snag a couple of anchorlines. Complain about everything; starting, of course, with the food. Remember the basic rule... "What is mine is mine; what is yours is mine too!" Pee in public as often as possible. Pretend that if you don't 'notice' yourself tossing your garbage overboard—then you haven't. Most of all: don't worry, be happy.

The crew of *Wild Card* for St. Barths Regatta:
Larry Best, Jim, Carolyn, Dave Dostal, and Foxy
of Jost Van Dyke

Sailing With Mister Macho

"Okay, honey," I said to my wife Carolyn as I watched the dark squall approaching directly ahead of us. "Let's get the jib rolled up. This squall looks like it could have a serious amount of wind in it. I'd rather be safe than sorry, and I don't want to stretch the sail..."

I glanced at my old friend Stevie LaRuzzo as Carolyn prepared to haul in on the tag line of the Harken roller furler on our jib. Stevie was looking uncomfortable; it was difficult for him to allow a woman to engage in strenuous physical activity in his presence without pitching in. He was an old fashioned, macho man—a former professional football player who was accustomed to playing by the old rules of male/female relationships.

My petite wife and he had already clashed a couple of times during our three day Caribbean cruise.

"Let's do it," I told Carolyn as I eased the boat up a couple of degrees higher on its course to relieve the tremendous pressure on the large headsail.

Carolyn started pulling in on the small Dacron tagline. There was quite a bit of strain on it, and she had to 'put her back into it' to make progress. Stevie watched for awhile, and then just couldn't resist. "Let me get it, honey," he said as he reached ahead of her hands to grasp the line.

Now Stevie is a big boy. He has got muscles on top of muscles. He prides himself on his gym-sculpted body—at least in every department but what's between his cauliflower ears.

I could see the look of irritation flick across my wife's face as he took over her assigned task.

So, just as soon as Stevie had a good grip on the line and Carolyn was shoved aside—I headed the boat back off the wind ever-so-slightly. Stevie, not being a sailor, didn't realize it.

"Okay, Stevie," I said with a broad wink to my wife, "let's get it in."

"Yep," he grunted, and put his full body into pulling on the line. His massive arms muscles flexed, his stout thighs pumped, his huge neck bulged—but nothing happened to the tagline. It was as if it was a small steel rod in his hand.

"For God sake's, Stevie," I shouted at him. "Get it in, *now!*"

Stevie grunted like a pig, and, much to my amazement, managed to actually get in a couple of feet before I 'cracked' the helm off another degree or two to stop him.

"Carolyn," I said pointedly, "I need this sail in *right now* or we're gonna lose it. I don't want to *talk about* it, I want it *done*. So *you* do it..!"

Carolyn leapt ahead of Stevie with a huge grin on her face. "That's okay *honey,"* she said, "I'll get the rest of it in."

The moment her dainty hand touched the line, I allowed the boat to ease up—and she began hand-over-handing in the line.

I glanced as Stevie. The look on his broad sweating face was a combination of utter horror and total amazement. What he was witnessing was, at least to him, impossible.

"How does she *do* that," he cried as he dove forward to give it another try.

This time we showed him no mercy. Carolyn let go, and I sharply jammed the nose of the boat down... and poor Stevie started to get slowly dragged forward... down the loo'ard side deck.... watching horrified as his massive fingers started getting closer and closer to its aluminum sheave. "I-can't-(gasp!)-hold-it," whimpered Stevie.

Carolyn bailed him out once again. This time Stevie didn't make a single move to stop her as she pulled in the rest of the sail.

Then the squall hit, and the rain came, and things got a little too exciting for awhile to concentrate on bedeviling poor ole Stevie.

I wasn't planning on telling Stevie what we'd done; but in the end I had to. He was just too crestfallen to endure. But we left him to stew in his own morose juices until later that evening. We were sitting around in a comfortable beach bar with our boat silhouetted by the setting sun while watching for the green flash—when I told him.

He started to get mad at first—I could tell by the way he started chewing his lips
—but he soon saw the humor of it. "Geez," he said. "I almost killed myself attempting to get that damn sail hauled in..."

"I was scared you were going to rip the forestay right out of the stemhead fitting..." I admitted.

"Buy me a drink, *honey?"* my wife Carolyn asked Stevie with a beautiful, impish grin.

"Barkeep!" Stevie bellowed, "Bring this *sailor* a drink!"

A Chartering Wife's "Hard Day at the Office"

Every working person—no matter what the profession—occasionally has a "tough day at the office." The men and women of the chartering industry are no different.

Most of the time, no one ever knows. The charter industry has a *Code of Silence* which is the envy of the Mafia. (A service industry in such intimate contact with its customers must, I suppose, exercise discretion.) Still, secrets are hard to keep in our little watery community. A few drinks—and loose lips sink ships.

This is especially true on St. Thomas and St. John. The sleazy reporters, informants, and stringers of *Caribbean Boating* are everywhere. Roll over a rock in the parking lot of Yeeck Haven, and we crawl out with our tape recorders whirling. Utter a few secret words at the Bilge Bar, or Bottom's Up, or The Back Yard... and soon the whole world knows about it.

I spend a *lot* of my life pretending to be a drunken lush—just to get some of these stories. Time and time again... I've put my liver on the line...

The very best Caribbean stories—of course—never see print. Too hot to handle. Too outrageous to be believed. Too strange for prime-time.

But every once in awhile, I hear a story which is so... typically Lush Tropical Vegetable-ish that I can't resist sharing it with my readers. This is one.

A large motor yacht was recently returning from Grenada with a group of six elderly charter guests.

Now these charter guests weren't merely old—they were ancient. All of them were in their late 80's and about half were already showing signs of acute rigor mortis. They spent most of their time gathered around the galley table with food stuck to their faces—discussing denture adhesives and burial insurance.

They were—one doesn't want to sound harsh, but one wants to be accurate—a pretty grim group.

Our charter crew—a husband/skipper, a wife/mate, and a cook—were handling everything very professionally... until the regular cook ran off with a Frenchman in Martinique.

They hired a new cook in Antigua.

Now the new cook turned out to be, at best, an alcoholic air-head without a grain of common sense in her bodacious body.

The wife had to accompany her everywhere ashore—and in the

galley she turned out to be a total disaster... ("Apparently the only thing she'd ever cooked or baked or smoked before were her own brain cells..!)

The wife had to take up the slack—and wasn't too pleased about it.

They proceeded northward, and anchored off a nice little island that was having a dance. The cooked demanded to go. (The charter guests never left the boat, preferring to stay in their bunks with the sheets pulled over their heads—and play hold-their-breath when anyone peered in to see if they were still alive...)

Anyway, the cook demanded to go ashore—and the wife thought it wise to accompany her.

The skipper—who would care for the guests while they were away—was suppose to pick them up in an hour or so.

Now the men at this dance weren't effete tourist dudes—on the contrary! They were young island fishermen out for a good time. And they hadn't seen two more beautiful creatures emerge from the sea in a long time.

They were soon swinging the women around the dance floor as if they were indestructible rag dolls and it was party/party/ party!

The skipper took a lot longer to pass around all the required pills, pillows, and platitudes than expected and it wasn't until rather late that he finally managed to take the dinghy ashore to retrieve his crew.

Now exactly what happened next—and why or how—isn't clear. But the captain had one single drink, and then turned into a werewolf.

Or close.

He started crawling around the floor. Barking. Cursing. Etc! (Whether he'd been slipped a Mickey or not is still unknown.)

The wife was horrified. Not only was the cook out of control, but now her 220-pound husband was howling at the moon!

The husband wouldn't return to the boat, the cook was 'dirty-dancing' with about 50 hopeful guys—and the wife was near tears.

Then the husband calmly laid down on the dance floor—and passed out.

The wife started to freak. She grabbed the cook, and they both attempted to drag the prone body of the skipper across the beach to the dinghy. It was slow going.

Finally, the biggest, nastiest, meanest looking of the fisherman grabbed a leg and lugged the skipper across the beach like he was an inflatable doll.

The women couldn't get the skipper into the dinghy, so the fisherman helped.

The fisherman, being a true gentleman, pointed out that they'd never get him onto the power yacht themselves...

So all four of them dinghied out to the boat. The fisherman tossed the skipper into the cockpit, but perhaps he wasn't gentle enough—because the skipper woke up... with a vengeance.

Now this skipper is normally the nicest, calmest, quietest guy in the world—but not tonight.

He awoke to a private nightmare—and immediately started cursing out his wife, his life, the guests—and the whole freak'n world at the top of his lungs.

There was nothing the poor wife could do or say to make him shut up.

He ranted on.

One of the ancient guests lurched aft from below, and complained she couldn't sleep because of all the noise.

The wife glued on her chartering smile, and pointed out that she was doing everything she could to shut up the captain.

"That's not the noise keeping us awake," said the old lady.

The wife dashed down below, rushed forward, and listened.

It sounded like the entire bow of the boat was being pounded like a drum by a sledge hammer...

...the wife ran on deck, rushed forward... and then averted her face from the fisherman and cook on the foredeck, screaming, "That does it! THAT DOES IT! This is TOOOO MUCCHH!!!!"

Hatches started opening, the fisherman started apologizing, the cook had a cigarette, the skipper asked what was up, the guests demanded more sleeping pills...

The next morning, when the wife went into the galley, there was the cook reading a recipe for scrambled eggs as if nothing had happened.

"I don't know whether to just fire you right here, or take you to the next island and give you a plane ticket back to Antigua," mused the wife.

"What?" said the cook. "Why? What are you talking about?"

"You don't remember?"

"No," said the cook.

So the wife explained exactly what had happened in as graphic, and cruel a manner as possible.

At the end, there was a moment of silence, and then the cook started screaming.

"Shut up, you FOOL!" yelled the wife at the top of her lungs. The hung-over skipper rolled out of his bunk, clutching his head in pain. The geriatric guests— neatly gathered at the galley table—were grinning from ear to ear....

...as the cook grabbed a scrub brush and a can of Kitchen Cleanser, and dove over the side of the boat screaming all the while. (Whether she was scared of NAVIGATIONAL AIDS or some other type was never clear...)

    The most amazing part of the story came at the end when the guests each tipped the crew quite heavily, and said they hadn't had such an "exciting vacation experience" in years....

Wild Card with a double-reefed main and the big jib

Sea Swine

Sometimes it seems as if every over-grown patrol boy with a hard-on for law enforcement has grabbed a tin badge, a stainless steel gun, and a high-powered outboard boat—and gone in search of some evil boaters to "bring to justice!"

This is particularly true in the U.S. Virgin Islands, where the term *probable cause* means that... if you are a member of the marine community... you are *probably* guilty of something.

The U.S. Coast Guard (USCG) is on the prowl constantly. They seem to delight in taking laws which are primarily intended to be applied to large ocean liners... and gleefully applying them to local folks in dinghies.

The USCG is currently attempting to force the local fishing boats to carry EPIRBs (Emergency Position Indicating Radio Beacons). They don't seem to realize that if the local West Indian skippers of these little fishing craft could afford to buy an EPIRB... they certainly wouldn't be risking their lives out at sea every day!

Of course, we should not solely single out the Feds. There are plenty of local law enforcement "wannabes" waiting in the goose-stepping wings should the USCG put away their guns and go home.

The Department of Planning and Natural Resources (DPNR) gives their 'enforcement officers' a very low wage, a couple of hours of instruction, and a large handgun—and then honestly expects them to enforce very complex environmental laws which many of them have not read nor understood.

There have been so many complaints lodged against the U.S. National Park Service on St. John recently that it is becoming something of a joke. (Most of the complaints have been lodged by mainland visitors—local residents are smart enough to keep a low profile until this bureaucratic hurricane blows itself out.)

Of course, the FBI has the right to board any vessel in US waters at any time for any reason... or, for that matter, any US vessel anywhere on the high seas. (The CIA pretends it doesn't exist in the Caribbean, so 'shhhhh!')

The USVI Police Department used to have a very intimidating, very aggressive marine 'Blue Lightning' narcotics strike force... but they 'disappeared' so much of the cocaine and drug money they confiscated... that a new (reform) police chief immediately announced he was 'disappearing' their organization upon taking office.

The USVI even has a special 'litter police' which (rarely, thankfully!) drives around town in new fancy government vehicles.

(Evidently, while on their way to pick up their government paychecks, they occasionally hassle small business owners about how they dispose of their trash.)

Of course, these are just some of the *cop shops* which have jurisdiction over you while in U.S. and/or Park waters. Don't forget the U.S. Customs Service. Or the U.S. National Immigration Service. Or the Environmental Protection Agency. Etc.

The Bureau of Alcohol, Tobacco and Firearms (ATF) have not been very active in the USVI so far—but who knows? After the Waco fiasco they surely could use some good press.

All of the above would be fairly funny if it wasn't so darn sad. The fact of the matter is that many of the boaters anchored in Long Bay regularly hear the sound of gunfire coming from the Paul M. Pearson housing projects just across the street to windward.

It is difficult for them as U.S. taxpayers to understand why all the law enforcement officials in the area have their backs turned to the gunfire—and are instead intently peering out into the harbor in hopes of finding a boater in an improperly lit dinghy or without a life jacket.

Occasionally it seems as if law enforcement in the U.S. has collectively given up on catching the *creeps* and has instead focused its stern attentions on the *populace.*

After all, they are easier to catch—and don't fire back when fired upon.

Weekending with the Wife and Kid

Every normal American male has a deep-seated desire to terrorize his wife and kids. I'm no exception. I receive a secret, sick, sadistic thrill by yelling at my wife and reprimanding my child. Of course, this isn't considered a cool thing to do *unless you own a boat.*

That's right: a husband and father has no right to abuse his family *but a CAPTAIN can be stern with his crew*! The simple act of owning a boat makes such utterly rude and totally obnoxious behavior perfectly acceptable. Any skipper can 'discipline' his crew anywhere anytime for any reason.

That's a fact. It's not only allowed, it's expected!

For many of us, Captain Bligh wasn't an overbearing, heartless, domineering jerk... but a wonderfully 'firm' sea-going role model. Let's face it, abusing your crew is, traditionally, one of the best parts of recreational boating.

When a boat is brand new, coaxing the wife and kids aboard is relatively easy. However, after the first few weekends of sea-going abuse, they tend to be rather hesitant to be piped back aboard for more of the same.

However, a determined skipper will have no real problem shaming his family back for more salt-stained misery.

First off, a skipper should bear in mind that he has *every right* to demand that his wife and kids accompany him on his weekend nautical jaunts. After all, his boat cost a small fortune and he only purchased it so that he could spend some 'quality time' with *them*, the ungrateful little land-leeches!

There, *that's* the proper attitude!

I recently spent Memorial Day weekend with my wife and child aboard our 38 foot sloop *Wild Card.* We cruised over to Jost Van Dyke.

It started out the way all good family outings do: "How'd you like to get away and relax for the weekend?" I asked my long-suffering wife.

How could she turn down such an innocent-sounding, gracious offer? "We'll have a blast," I assured her. "You get some supplies while I get the boat ready..."

Thus, I made sure that our vessel's bunks were still soft and comfortable as she trudged all over town buying provisions; mostly beer, wine, rum, and ice.

I didn't start the actual abuse until *after* we'd cast off our mooring— in fact, I waited a generous number of seconds before beginning to shout an endless stream of confusing and contradictory orders...

"Hoist up the mainsail; cast off the keel!. Look lively, you idiot! DON'T FOUL THE HALYARDS! Smartly, now! Faster! Easy now! Slow... HEAVE-HO! Oh, no... DON'T LET THE BATTENS GET CAUGHT ON THE TOPPING LIFT..!

Once out to sea, it might have appeared to a casual observer that I was just lying back in the cockpit of my yacht, '...lim'n away de day, mon!'

But the truth was far from that. I was watching my crew like a hawk, searching for the slightest mistake as they tended the jib sheets, polished the brass, cleaned the cockpit floor, and kept a steady stream of crispy salted snacks flowing out of the sweltering galley. (My kid worked the cooler, took the drink orders, and acted as waitress.)

Whenever either of them appeared to be starting to enjoy themselves, I'd stir things up by shouting, "Tacking! Coming-about! Cast off! Sheet in! Grind/grind/grind!" just to make sure they were on their collective toes.

Once ashore, I allowed them to clear into Customs and Immigration while I sucked down a few (and a few more) Pina Coladas at *Foxy's*.

They arrived at the bar just in time to pay my bulging tab. (My eyes were having a wee-bit of trouble focusing, so I thought it best if they handled all the financial matters.)

Then it was back to sea, and the hard slog to windward to Green Cay. We were all hot and sweaty by the time we arrived at our new anchorage, so I allowed them to dive over the side... and scrape the barnacles off the unpainted hull of my slovenly watercraft.

There were only a few thousand barnacles tenaciously attached, and thus it only took a couple of hours to get the job done *right.*

Of course, watching all this physical activity and delegating all these 'shipboard tasks' can give a man a pretty healthy appetite.

They soon cooked up quite a gourmet meal, despite the fact that the boat was rolling from rail to rail, the stove had no fiddles to keep the pots in place, and that most of the food aboard came from expanded cans. (Rusty tins of botulism are always *cheap!)*

Hauling up the anchor to sail home was, at least for me, the high point of the cruise.

I didn't coddle my crew by cranking up the engine or allowing them to use the anchor windlass.

Instead I had them pull us (all ten tons of us) directly into the twenty knot breeze, and then attempt to snatch out the well-buried anchor by pure brute force.

I sincerely hoped that they'd be able to do it alone, without my muscular assistance, but I was wrong. I had to make it a team effort during the most critical part. "Put your *backs* into it, you FARMERS," I shouted loudly from the cockpit. "Pull, don't just TALK about it! I

WANT THAT ANCHOR UP NOW, LADIES... NOW, NOW, NOOWWWW, DAMN IT!!!!!!"

In order to shout effectively, I'd had to put down my drink and cup both hands around my rubbery lips. Only then were they able to catch the proper sense of urgency.

Almost immediately the anchor came flying up out of the water like a turbo-charged yo-yo, dramatically proving the effectiveness of my strenuous physical actions.

During the rest of the trip home, I pretty much rested on my laurels while my wife rubbed suntan lotion on my back and my kid wrote pathetic begging letters ("I'm hungry!") to all of our close relatives.

I'll admit my own sailing performance wasn't flawless: I should NOT have told them to grab the mooring pennant as we flew by it at seven knots under full sail.

But all is well that ends well, and their both being squeezed through the narrow forward hawse hole slowed us down enough so that I was able to snatch the bloody mooring pennant with my boathook as it drifted by the cockpit.

"Boy, that was a SWELL weekend," I told members of the St. Thomas Rescue's Sea Recovery Team who were soon buzzing dangerously close to my boat as they plucked what was left of the wife and kid out of the harbor to rush them to the hospital. "There's nothing like a weekend cruise with the family to *relax* you!"

Cap'n Fatty on *Wild Card* with
Carolyn and Roma and a urinal

That Sinking Feeling

Sinking is no fun. I've learned this lesson the hard way. "Sinking is," my wife noted wearily one morning as she waded ashore as our floating home ceased to, "...sinking is a *damp* shame!"

Despite this, I'm a vastly experienced sinker. I've sunk large schooners, small sloops, and medium-sized power vessels. (I don't even *count* losing vessels under 20 feet!) I've had numerous boats attempt to scuttle themselves the moment I stepped aboard. A few have decided, after only a couple of hours of my demented hand on their trembling helm, that suicide was their best option.

I sunk one boat *twice!* (Luckily, it *stayed* sunk on the second attempt.)

The realization that the vessel I am on is sinking always comes to me as a horribly rude shock. I'll be sailing along, and suddenly notice that the boat is a tad sluggish. "I wonder why *that* is?" I'll think to myself. Then I'll notice that the surface of the ocean appears a bit closer than normal—and that the bow is drunkenly plunging into the wave troughs—and that the leeward rail is so far underwater that barnacles are starting to grow upon it...

Suddenly, the dim light-bulb of partial enlightenment will slowly go off over my dull-witted head. "Perhaps we're sinking," I'll muse to myself.

Then I'll peer down the companionway at my floating floorboards. "By gosh, we *are* sinking," I'll mutter, basking in the glory of having, once again, proven myself to be absolutely, totally correct.

The first thing I generally do whilst sinking is to switch on the bilge pumps. This enables the discarded bras, half-eaten pizzas, and used condoms sloshing around in the oily water belowdecks to immediately clog the gurgling intake hoses.

This gives the boat a 'sporting chance' to sink if it so desires.

Of course, by the time I realize we are in serious danger of really-sinking-for-true, my ship's batteries are usually far underwater. This eliminates those embarrassing 'May Day! calls which are so damaging to one's self-image.

I was only a 'wee child' when the first major vessel slid out from under me. It was my father's 52 foot Alden schooner *Elizabeth.* This was in the late 1950's. We were in a hurricane, and attempting to anchor in the lee of a deserted island in the Gulf of Mexico.

The moment our keel struck the sandbar, I knew it was the beginning of the end.

Picture being inside an old wooden boat at night... in the middle of a full-fledged, furious hurricane... and having your boat picked up and tossed a hundred feet through the ocean spume by a huge wave... and then dropped onto (seemingly) solid concrete... again and again and again.

It was not a nice feeling.

My mother gathered together all the lifejackets aboard, strapped each of them laboriously to her body & her arms & her legs... and then jammed our single life ring over her head... and climbed up on the galley table... and began screaming at the top of her lungs as the boat filled with icy cold water.

After that horrific experience at such an impressionable age—most of my other sinkings have been, well, almost *boring*.

At the age of sixteen (1968) I was crossing Lake Michigan in my 22 foot double-ended Atkin's sloop *Corina* when she suddenly began to take on a serious amount of water. Of course, it was night—it always is when you're fighting for your life upon an ocean's wave.

I pumped all night. I was barely keeping up with it. At dawn I was amazed to observe (by leaning precariously over the side of my boat) that the aft edge of my keel appeared to be pulled away from my deadwood by almost 10 inches.

I could see blue water (and keel bolts) between by boat and its massive lead keel!

"Gee," I idly wondered. "If the keel drops off, I wonder which will sink me first —the holes from the missing keel bolts or the instantaneous capsize?"

It was enough to make even a pimply-faced teenager shudder. Both the boat and I eventually managed to reach shore relatively intact—but neither of us were ever quite 'right' again.

Once I allowed a 36 foot ketch I'd just built to partially sink because I'd forgotten to close one of two seacocks while winterizing my engine. The good news was that I'd discovered my error before the boat settled to the bottom; the bad news was that I'd drowned my brand new diesel engine, and boxes and boxes of new electronics which I hadn't even gotten around to installing yet.

When your boat gets wet, so does your wallet.

Fifteen years later, that same boat was holed and driven ashore in Culebra during Hurricane Hugo. I and my family went out the companionway as the water came in through the holes in the bottom.

Once again, my wallet got soaked.

I've begun to think of my boats as large, expensive yo-yos which go up-and-down of their own free will. If I'm lucky, I live in them; if I'm not, lobsters and moray eels live in 'em!

The only thing I can say (weakly) in my own defense is that I've never really 'lost' a boat. They sink, but I always know exactly *where*.

This is cold comfort, I know, but at least it's something. And all this s(t)inking misery I've suffered has finally produced some new design thinking—my new 'dream boat' will have hidden nylon liftbags built right into the chainplates.

If that ain't progress, what is?

Cap'n Fatty on a boat he didn't sink

A Sailor Sleeps Ashore

I am 43 years of age, and have lived aboard various sailing craft for over 35 of those years. I have no ambition to live ashore, even under the coziest of circumstances. I am, to put it mildly, a confirmed boater and a die-hard live-aboard.

However, I am also a family man. This requires a certain amount of pragmatic flexibility. Thus when my wife (of 25 years) and my daughter (of 14) recently asked me (longingly) if we could 'house-sit' for the summer—I reluctantly agreed.

We ended up in a spacious mansion. It is huge. It has multi-levels, buildings, and cisterns. It consumes about as much electricity as Manhattan. It came to us complete with cars, cats, and pool toys. I've stayed in national hotels with fewer bedrooms. Just the Jacuzzi is bigger than many marinas I've sailed into.

Of course, the people who lent us the place for the summer are perversely insane. Why else would anyone give a huge, pristine mansion to a family of salt-stained sailing slobs—all of whom have never swept a floor, cleaned a pool, or mowed a lawn in their entire *lives!*

The first night I spend ashore was completely horrible. I was totally out of my natural nautical element. For the first few days I thought that all the toilets in the house had the smallest, *dumbest* pump handles imaginable!

Eventually, in order to get some sleep, I put on my foul weather jacket and laid in a bath tub while cold water dripped on me—and immediately fell asleep. (It wasn't *exactly* like being offshore, but it was close.)

Bugs, bugs, BUGS! They are everywhere ashore. Moths. Ants. Spiders. Worms. Mosquitos. Flies. Sandfleas. No-see-ums. And to top it all off—giant flying cockroaches as large as small brown dogs!

How can anyone live ashore? I mean, REALLY! It's filthy. Dirt is everywhere; in fact, people actually construct their houses on dirt, and then spend the rest of their lives attempting to keep it out. *Stupid!*

If the bugs and the dirt weren't bad enough, there are the large wild animals which freely roam the countryside.

One evening, while my wife and I were, er... snuggling. A wild donkey stuck its head into our open bedroom window and brayed loudly. I was shocked, and for a few (delicious) moments thought that my wife had a primitive, animalistic side which I'd only just discovered.

Wild animals aren't the only things roaming the countryside. People do it too. They just drop in. Unannounced. Hungry. Thirsty. Talkative.

It's horrible. They just show up, smile—and there goes all your food and booze!

The whole house constantly hums with electrical activity, like a giant factory. Dozens of motors, pumps, and machines turn on and off at will—their will, of course, not mine.

The kitchen is the worst portion of the house for me. It contains a multitude of dicing, slicing, and disemboweling machines. Nothing makes it out of this area alive.

It took us about a week to locate the low-tech gas stove. It was completely buried under electric blenders, can openers, bread machines, slicers, liquefies, skillets, toasters, roasters, browners, broilers, grillers, and nukers. (Both these appliances and anything which issues from them tend to make me physically ill. I prefer *heating* my food, not *bombing* it!)

If all this wasn't enough distraction, there is the incessant ubiquitous telephone. This is a relatively modern instrument of torture which wealthy landlubbers rent by the month to punish themselves for having too much money.

This phone rings like a metronome. There are people at the other end of it, and they want answers *fast!* (Unfortunately, they have far more questions than I've got answers, and this was beginning to be a serious problem until I Crazy-glued the answering machine to 'on', and gleefully tossed all the micro-recording cassettes down the snarling garbage disposal.)

Thus I spend my summer. A lot of my time is spent lying around the Jacuzzi on the sundeck—bemoaning the fact that I have to walk a couple of feet to the ice machine/bar each time I want another pitcher of Pina Coladas.

Life can be tough, especially ashore.

But what I do most of the time is to count the days left before I can move back aboard my beloved *Wild Card*.

Living aboard, especially here in the Virgins, is a wonderful lifestyle. My boat has no telephone, no cable TV, no VCR, no electronic/nuclear kitchen. There is always plenty of beach 'parking places' for my dinghy. Solar cells provide our electrical needs. We do not have, nor want, an inboard engine.

My boat is surrounded by a wide expanse of salt water, and thus is well-insulated from dirt, bugs, donkeys, friends, family, salesmen, creeps, teefs, and jerks—and all the other modern vexations of shoreside living.

My boat may not be heaven, but it is often very close.

Some people would be horrified at how tiny she is—but we view her to be as 'huge as the horizon.' Example: our swimming pool is the largest in the world. Each evening our cockpit is filled with a million stars. Each day there is plenty of tropical wind to fill our billowing sails.

There seems to be a certain cosmic sense to the live-aboard lifestyle, a certain ecological balance, a certain rational basis for our fun, free-wheeling, salt-stained ways.

And so this September when I return to my modest vessel—it will be with much glee and not a backwards glance towards the shore. Sure, I realize that someone has to live in the dirt on land—but I thank my lucky (navigational) stars it isn't me or my family. Each to his own. It's the sailing life for us!

The Goodlanders with Lulu Magras of St. Barths at his farmhouse in France

Virgin Anchor Wars

The anchorages of the Virgin Islands are getting kinda crowded. Often it is difficult to tell if the anchorage is just full—or all the boats are rafted up. Live-aboard boaters in Red Hook, St. Thomas are being forced to anchor so far out of the harbor that they are leaving their dinghies in Cruz Bay, St. John.

You can now walk from Leinster Bay, St. John to Soper's Hole, Tortola most days—if you're willing to clamber across all those sidedecks, through all the cockpits, and over all the lifelines to get there. (Sir Francis Drake's channel has been rerouted north of Jost Van Dyke.)

Yeah, it is crowded, and getting more crowded every day. The moment a patch of water appears, another shoddy boat is hastily built to fill it. People are anchoring so far offshore that on hazy days they can't even see it.

This has forced the average VI yachtsmen to be flexible, to change with the changing times. Instead of heartily welcoming cruising sailors into his anchorage as he's traditionally done, he is now forced to discourage them.

This is being done in a number of subtle ways. The first line of defense is the GLARE. The moment another vessel hoves into sight, the VI yachtsman rushes up on deck and GLARES at it intently—while doing threatening isometric exercises upon his weapon-strewn cabintop. (Muttering, throwing rocks, and/or urinating towards the intruding vessel often adds a deft touch of discouragement.)

The next step is to whip the tarpaulin off the foredeck machine gun.

These 'spray-guns' are fast becoming standard equipment on many of the local boats. A growing number of anchor windlass companies are now providing stock 'universal' stainless steel machine gun sockets as standard equipment on their newer models.

If all of the above fails to discourage the approaching vessel, it is time to deploy your special 'repel boarders' fenders to protect your topsides. These fenders (sometimes called 'French fenders' by the non-French) are made out of stout planks with outward-pointing rail-road spikes driven through them. While deploying these, it is best to yell Creole obscenities while ranting something like, "So ya wanna raft up, do ya..?"

Needless to say, almost anything is fair to ward off unwanted territorial aggression. Some yachtsmen draw the line at having Exocet missiles mounted underneath their spreaders, but a growing minority of them seem to find the heat-seeking rockets somewhat comforting.

Wiring your power-hailer directly into your mega-bass boom box is a good idea, but deafness is becoming such a serious problem among our youth that this isn't going to be much of a deterrent in the near future.

Flaming arrows still work, as do flare guns, hydraulic slingshots, and spearguns. Pan-handling is losing its shock value, but pretending to be a religious fanatic while waving around a dog-eared copy of *The Watch Tower* will still make many boaters sheer away immediately.

A few of the longterm live-aboards have gone to extreme lengths to ensure their privacy. One fellow, just after Hurricane Hugo, purchased a dozen broken masts from various wrecked boats. He has just the tops of these poking above the surface of the water around his boat—and his loud threats to sink anyone who anchors remotely close are taken quite seriously indeed.

Others hang dead animals, decapitated mannequins, and/or posters of Charles Manson in their rigging to discourage new arrivals. Flying a Nazi flag as a yacht ensign can have a similar dampening effect.

Of course, nothing can discourage a bareboater. They are a breed apart—fearless to the point of oblivion! There is no such concept as 'too crowded' to them.

Recently a 48 foot bareboat came into a crowded anchorage so forcefully that two 24 foot boats popped out like pumpkin seeds.

Which isn't to say that all the anchorages in the Virgins are always crowded. That isn't true. About once a year, the Tourism department empties a bay or two to take some picturesque 'empty anchorage, deserted beach photographs in Paradise' to entice even more visitors to the islands.

The official line seems to be the more the merrier, but those boaters intending to anchor on the western side of the Virgins should brush up on their Spanish, and a few simple Dutch phrases might come in handy for those intending to drop the hook on the eastern side...

Great Cruz Bay, St. John, Virgin Islands

The Savage Realities of Yacht Deliveries

Delivering massive mega-yachts to various watery destinations on this planet is a difficult, serious business which requires great skill, courage, and competence.

At least that's what we tell our 'owners.'

Of course, the reality is quite different. Those of us in the marine community who regularly deliver vessels between New England and Paradise primarily do so for one simple reason: it's fun.

I love getting paid to break other people's boats.

When I'm first approached about a delivery, the aspect I'm most interested in is 'depth'. Not the depth of the vessel, but the financial depth of the vessel's owner. I have *my* accountant call *his* accountant—and get a guarantee that the money pipeline couldn't & wouldn't be interrupted by mere global war, world-wide famine, or any natural planetary disaster.

I mean, when I'm being arrested in the Royal Bermuda Snot Club for throwing the pool table (it's on the second floor) into the swimming pool (it's *not!*)—I don't want to worry about my owner's check bouncing on my very proper British bail bondsman, now do I? "...say wot, Ole Boy!"

Of course, I learned long ago never to allow myself to be talked into being 'captain'. No way! Captains have to accept responsibility. They have to 'go down with the ship' both literally and figuratively. They even have to pee into little plastic bottles. Even worse, at the end of the passage they have to attempt to justify where all the money went. Even the most creative, convincing liar can have grave difficulties in this critical final phrase of the scam... er, I mean, delivery.

Generally speaking, captains are the lowest IQ members aboard, stupidly willing to accept all the blame without significant recompensation. Delivery crews instinctively realize this, and often secretly agree among themselves to 'divorce' the skipper at the first sign of serious shoreside trouble. "Feed 'em to the landsharks!" is the idea.

Seasoned delivery crews always carry their passports, a condom, and hundred dollar bill stashed in their watertight money belt at all times. (Heading northward, it's a good idea to include an anti-drug pamphlet produced by the DEA and a signed color photo of President George Bush; going southward, a collection of Adelbert Bryan's speeches and a photo of Nelson Mandela framed in ganja leaves can't hurt!)

The most rewarding & creative job on a delivery is the bookkeeping. A dozen cases of Stoli/Mount Gay/Jack Daniels gets reimbursed as 'lubrication'. Cute new crew uniforms with matching sun hats are deducted under "tropical crew covering cloth apparatuses." The porn videos, cans of caviar, and bottles of Dom are all handled in a similar manner.

Many newcomers to the delivery game balk at such thin deceptions. "Our owners can't be *that* dumb," they claim.

"Yeah?" replies the Old Crusty Salt, "Well, if they're so smart, how come they're paying *us* a small fortune to party our little guts out on the very same mega yacht that they haven't got the time to barely even visit—because they're too busy getting ulcers & committing suicide while attempting to pay for it all..."

The most important part of any delivery is just getting away from the dock—with the bulging box of petty cash and the sheaf of charge cards. Once you cast off, the whole world is your oyster. Bringing a Feadship from Yacht Haven to Newport Yachting Service can take many months—especially if you have to stop in Mexico and the Azores for spare parts!

It's best to avoid all contact with your owner; however, if you *must* speak—whine!

Complain about how fuzzy the display is on the interactive GPS system, how long it takes to get a dial tone on the sat-telephone link up, how noisy the dishwasher is, how ashamed you are about only having two 300hp jet-skis...

In essence, lay a heavy guilt trip on them. Extremely wealthy people are generally pretty gracious about accepting guilt. They are used to handling a lot of it. It is sort of their job, in a way.

The trip from St. Thomas to Newport is easy. Keep the wind on the starboard side of your vessel for the first few days, and then follow the jet-trails into Bermuda. (Where did you think all those 747s were landing—on an air craft carrier?)

Once you're stern-to the dock at either Hamilton or St. George's—spending large sums of your owner's money should be relatively easy. Those long figures on the local merchandise aren't stock numbers—those are the prices. No, not in francs or pesos—that's US dollars!!!

I usually head straight for the Hog's Penny Pub. Some of the best memories I can't recall have taken place there.

The passage between Bermuda and Long Island Sound can be a bit more dicey. But the important thing is to make sure that your 'owner' realizes that you are risking *your very life* to take special care of his largest, most expensive material possession.

No voyage is complete without a few little 'fun-fibs' about a man-overboard situation with a hungry shark, being attacked by Jamaican pirates, or strafed by a squadron of angry Iraqi aircraft...

If your owner solicitously says things like, "...well, at least no one was killed or injured!" then you got him where you want him.

No matter how calm the conditions are when you cross the Gulfstream—claim that you almost lost the vessel when you were hit by a "...locally heavy hurricane that the NOAA forecasters completely missed..!"

Just to add a little credence to the gag, I usually run ropes from the foredeck anchor windlass aft to the stantions, cockpit dodger tubing, radar mounts, fog horns, sat/nav antennas, and compass pedestals...

...I don't rip them clean off the deck, merely take a healthy strain on them. When they tilt over at about a 45 degree angle, that's perfect!

How could your owner now dare to doubt your scary sea stories—backed up by such irrefutable physical evidence? From all the partying you did in Bermuda, chances are you're gonna look like death-warmed-over anyway. The double whammy gets 'em every time!

Not a jury on the Eastern Seaboard would convict you!

Please bear in mind that this isn't just idle speculation on my part—I've done all this (and worse!) *many* times in the last couple of decades. I've crewed on dozens of boats heading up, and dozens of boats heading down—but never both. (I think maybe the ones I bring up still ain't out of the boat yard in the spring...)

Don't ever feel the remotest twinge of guilt—the fact is that you are providing two excellent services for the mega-yacht owner.

First, you're moving his vessel from Point A to Point B.

Second, the main reason mega-yacht owners are mega-yacht owners is so that they will be asked that all important question, "How much does a boat like this cost?"

After partaking of your services, they'll feel completely justified in replying, "If you have to ask, you can't afford it!"

A Strange and Twisted Tale
of the Captain & Crew

My buddy Bobby is a fun loving kind of guy. He's got long sun-drenched blond hair, big muscles, and an open, honest smile. He likes to party, likes to play—and he loves 'the ladies'. He also loves to sail.

He's one of those easy-going heart-of-gold fellows who... how shall I say it... doesn't spend a lot of time mulling over the larger questions of life. He's 'uncomplicated,' if you get my drift.

He's also a USCG licensed captain—and works in the charter trade. He especially likes skippering big, powerful sailing vessels, and I guess he's pretty good at it. He's chartered out of Red Hook, Road Town, Sint Maarten, and Antigua—and had some pretty nice boats under his command.

The vessels he's in charge of always gleam, he usually gets paid pretty well, and everybody is usually pretty happy.

No sweat.

The only problem is that Bobby often falls in love—like a couple of times a week. He genuinely loves every women he meets—regardless of race, creed, color, size, or temperament—and can't seem to prevent himself from succumbing to their many charms.

Life's a candy store to Cap'n Bobby—and he has an incurable sweet tooth.

Hey, why not, right?

Anyway, everything was going along pretty good a few years back—when he met Carole Ann down in Bequia.

It was instant love at first sight (and lust, too)—and Carole Ann was soon working as cook and mate for Cap'n Bobby.

They cruised down to Venezuela, and did the ABC islands. They worked Antigua, and then Sint Maarten, and ended up back in Red Hook.

They were quite a 'marine unit' for a winter's charter season. For a long time, it was as close to bliss as Bobby ever got.

Then, trouble started. First it was just an occasional rain squall in Carole Ann's eyes, then a few storms—and soon Carole Ann was giving him daily gales of abuse.

It seems that her complaint was that he just drifted through life—just took it as it came. He didn't push, didn't hustle to get ahead.

"Why don't you *make* something of yourself," she blurted out to Bobby.

Bobby's feeling were hurt. He reckoned he'd already had. He made close to 50 grand a year, laid around in the sun all day, and never got too uptight. What more could a man ask for? (Like the Dire Strait's song says: "...money for nutt'n, and the chicks for free!")

"Don't you want to own a boat like this someday yourself?" she asked him—and Bobby looked at her like she was nuts.

"Of course not," Bobby said. "The owner gets to enjoy it about two weeks a year, and I get to enjoy it all the rest of the time. He *pays* full-time, and I *plays* full time. What would I want to own the damn thing for?"

Well, gradually their relationship started to crumble. Their minds drifted apart. They still loved each other—but Carole Ann wanted a man of action, power, and prestige... and all Cap'n Bobby wanted was Carole Ann... or somebody similar.

At the end of the season, Carole Ann went to the Big Apple for a month. It stretched to six weeks, and then Bobby got a card from her in L.A. A few months after that, she called from a hotel room in Monte Carlo, and said she was planning on skiing in the Alps for awhile...

Eventually, Cap'n Bobby lost track of her. There were many more fish in the sea—and he was able to blunt his loss. He'd heard that she'd married a rich industrialist from the Midwest... but he wasn't sure if it was true.

Her picture got pasted into one of his dog-eared ship's logs... along with the faces of many other young women he'd loved... a couple of which he'd already forgotten the names of.

He worked as a sport fishing captain in Cozumel for awhile, and did a Pacific delivery.

Then the Ultimate Job came along. He was hired to go to Finland and bring back a brand new 60 foot sailing vessel. The owner (a retired real estate investor from Michigan) wanted Cap'n Bobby to make sure it was in St. Barts for Christmas—so he and his new bride could honeymoon aboard. "It's a wedding present for her," the guy said.

Cap'n Bobby got the boat there on time, all right, and even managed not to pass out as Carole Ann strolled calmly up the gangplank. Despite the intervening years, she still didn't look half bad. "...And you must be Cap'n Bobby," she said shyly...

...and it was all he could manage to mumble, "Welcome aboard."

Bobby reports things are going pretty good—as well as can be expected, he guesses. But nothing is perfect, and everyone everywhere has at least a few problems. "Good male boat chefs..." Bobby says, sadly shaking his sun-drenched blond head, "They're hard to find..."

Gustavia, St. Barths, French West Indies

Dese Hurricanes
Mash up De Islands, Mon

Culebra after Hurricane Hugo - September 1989

Facing Marilyn Afloat

My deepest fear going into Hurricane Marilyn wasn't that I would once again lose my vessel and everything I owned—as I did during Hurricane Hugo in 1989—but that the storm would, once again, recast me into the pitiful role of 'hurricane storm victim'.

The most difficult part of a major hurricane isn't the actual storm; it is its messy aftermath. The storm itself is fairly exhilarating; it is its long term social and personal repercussions that are so wearying and ultimately devastating to its victims.

I remember the worst part of Hugo, at least for my family. It took place about ten days after the actual eye passed over us. My disheveled wife came to me and said grimly, "I don't mind being homeless and having lost everything we ever owned... but now we're starting to lose control of our lives, Fatty, *that* scares me—that scares me bad!"

That's what being homeless is all about. Powerlessness. There is nowhere you can go without someone's 'kind' permission. Even the simplest, most basic things become extremely difficult: washing, brushing your teeth, going to the bathroom.

When you are homeless there is nowhere left where you have any special rights, any special privileges. You are, potentially, everyone and anyone's victim.

It is a horrible, totally demoralizing feeling.

Two weeks after Hurricane Hugo, my wife, child, and I were spending the night in a fancy rental unit (with the 'kind' permission of the rental agent)—when its wealthy stateside owner returned unexpected and unannounced.

He was outraged to find a group of storm-ravaged 'squatters' on his property without his express permission. He berated us loudly as he ordered us to leave: we hopped around in the darkness of the bedroom, half naked, illuminated by his cruelly bobbing flashlight... as we attempted to get dressed and explain our wretched situation at the same time.

Intellectually, I understand his actions. He had 'every right', so to speak. But deep in my guts I'll always hate the son of a bitch—for treating my wife and child like stray dogs, and for how we were forced by circumstance to unflinchingly absorb his abuse without the slightest complaint nor retaliation.

That's what being homeless is all about: fearfully clutching your soiled clothes to your quaking chest in the middle of the night as some selfish moron treats you like a piece of... dirt.

And so, as Hurricane Marilyn approached, I prayed to the fickle wind gods that she would not treat us as harshly as her brother Hugo had, almost exactly six years ago to the day.

We spent Hurricane Marilyn aboard our 38 foot sloop *Wild Card* in Hurricane Hole, St. John, USVI—spider-webbed to the mangroves, with nine stout anchors down, our collective hearts in our throats.

My wife and child were aboard with me, just as they had been in Hugo. Once again, I'd asked them to ride it out ashore, and once again they'd refused. (I must admit that their refusal always both pleases and scares me.)

Like most Virgin Islanders, we thought the storm would be of relatively small consequence. But a couple of hours after dark, I realized that we were once again in a fight for our lives.

The wind was howling like the lost souls of a million drowned sailors. The air and the water and the spray were slowly merging into one. Large trees were snapping off the mountain ridge ahead of us—like fragile matchsticks. The motion inside the boat was becoming increasingly violent.

It was, once again, as if Satan was loose upon the sea.

In order to successfully survive a major hurricane afloat, a number of diverse factors must fall into place. 1.) You must be in a landlocked safe harbor that offers 360 degree protection from the sea and affords some shelter from the wind. 2.) You must have the proper hurricane anchoring gear (which few boats do). 3.) Both you and your neighbors must deploy all your gear properly, well before the storm strikes. 4.) You must get lucky (or at lease avoid being unlucky).

"Aye, matey! There's the rub!" as a laughing pirate might ruefully say. "Luck enters into it, like, *big time!*"

No matter how well prepared you are, your vessel will be lost if another vessel drags down on it. Or someone's roof gets caught sideways in your rig. Or an airborne jeep lands on your bow...

Yes, there are a million ways to lose your boat in 120 knots of wind, and many of them are beyond your control. That's the reality of the situation, regardless of what we sailors might like to believe. In the end, it's a crapshoot. And we're playing for high stakes: our boats, our homes, our families, and our own self-respect.

Hurricanes make winners and losers of us all, without regard to any logic or justice. Good people occasionally suffer; evil ones sometimes profit. It is enough to make you weep, and often does in the storm's aftermath.

We didn't listen to our VHF marine radio much during Marilyn—I preferred the evil entertainment of God's immense wrath just outside our companionway door. Besides, the radio was too depressing; listening to our friends lose their homes, break their bones, and watch their spouse's drown.

My *second* biggest worry was that the boat on my port side would break loose and crush ours like an eggshell. It could happen quick, really quick, so quick we might not have time to escape. We'd be trapped inside... as our boat was crushed... and we'd become entombed... in our sinking boat... on our way to a watery grave.

How would the water feel as it rose up around our necks, started lapping into our twitching nostrils, splashing into our gasping mouths..?

I was especially worried about the boat on my port side because it was a large wooden schooner—just like the stately vessel which had dragged into us during Hugo—and it seemed as if it might be our cosmic destiny to suffer the same sorry fate at the hands of the same type of vessel.

My *biggest* fear was that I'd break lose, and crush the lovely wooden sloop on my starboard side. It was a fragile craft, and much beloved by its fastidious owner. He'd rebuilt it over the course of a dozen long, hard years. He'd lavished all of his money, time, tears and talent on it.

And now it was directly to leeward of me, totally at our mercy. If the half inch dockline attached to my aft port cockpit winch broke—it would be toothpicks and damp sawdust before I could utter the pathetically ineffectual word 'sorry!'

The worst of the storm came in the middle of the night, at its darkest hour. This is always the case. Always.

Going on deck was becoming increasing difficult at that point. Still, we did it. We literally clawed our way forward. The wind seemed intent on plucking us off the deck. The rain drove into our faces like nails.

We checked our chafing gear, adjusted the tension on our anchor rodes, and inspected our mangrove lines. There wasn't much we could do—our efforts were almost laughably puny in the face of the powerful storm—but we did our best for whatever it was worth.

At dawn, the storm had abated enough (gusting to, say, only 50 knots) to begin moving around the anchorage via our 25 hp outboard dinghy.

We checked on our friends. It was grim work.

There were, of course, the winners and the losers. Twenty-four boats were ashore in Coral Bay; nearly as many were in the mangroves of Hurricane Hole. But the most shocking storm news was further to the west. St. Thomas and Culebra had taken an even harder hit than we had.

While the majority of vessels in our harbors survived, the majority of the vessels in many of the harbors on St. Thomas did not.

It was difficult to believe the reports we were hearing. With each new report, we'd shake our collective heads in disbelief, as if by rattling our brains we could somehow shake some sense into them. Could this many boats really have been lost? Could this many of our fellow sailors really have drowned?

It was slowly dawning on us. This was no little storm. It was worse than Hugo in nearly every measurable aspect; more deaths, more dollars, more tears.

The *Point Ledge*, our local US Coast Guard (USCG) vessel, hadn't been calmly responding to MAYDAYS during the long, storm-tossed night—but excitedly issuing them. Its final resting place after the hurricane—right in the middle of the busiest highway on St. Thomas—seemed to symbolize the entire disarray of the USVI marine community.

If the USCG's stoutest ship couldn't survive the storm, how could poor mom and pop aboard *Lazy Daze* be expected to?

The most enjoyable part of the whole ordeal for me (if such a concept has any validity at all) — took place a few days after the storm. I chopped the two dozen lines holding my beloved *Wild Card* to the mangroves and went sailing.

Just for the hell of it.

Wild Card seemed particularly alive—aquiver with excitement at once again being at sea. She eagerly dipped and curtsied to the ocean swells—her sails sang with joy as they were smartly hoisted.

And mine was the only sail in sight—from Virgin Gorda to Jost Van Dyke to St. Thomas to St. Croix.

We were all alone—and despite the misery we'd just left—it seemed as if the world had been scrubbed clean.

The most depressing moment for many of us in the Hurricane Hole area came via the VHF radio. It was just after dawn. The storm was still subsiding. A distressed boater, a middle-aged American man from the sound of his steady, educated voice, was calling VISAR. (VISAR is the BVI Search and Rescue Operation which had been such a comfort to all of us during the storm.)

"VISAR," the voice said, and then began to crack and gasp and weep... "VISAR..."

Even though I couldn't hear anything for awhile, I could tell that the man was silently crying, blubbering really, and didn't even realized that he still had his microphone keyed open.

"VISAR," he blubbered forlornly. "Could you tow me off..? Bring me pumps..? I'm hard aground... and sunk against the mangroves.... and my boat has a hole in it... VISAR, are you there? PLEASE?"

His plaintive wail—so heart-felt and immediately impossible—totally silenced the marine airwaves. He could have been any one of us. Any one of us could have been him. The fury of the storm had reduced him to the level of a crying child— he wanted VISAR to find his mommy... who would kiss his boo-boo... and make it all better.

But many of those of us listening knew—as he would soon be forced to realize— that there was no one who could 'kiss and make it better'.

There was only a lot of blood, sweat, and tears—and the long, difficult road to recovery ahead.

Salvors and Saviors

After Hurricane Marilyn, I became addicted to refloating boats. It was highly satisfying work. We always cheered as a boat slid off into deep water. It was almost impossible not to shout with joy—it seemed as if we were literally breathing life back into the stranded vessels.

One minute the wrecked boat would be a large, dead, useless object upon the unmoving, uncaring shore—and the next moment it would be alive upon the quivering sea.

We always swaggered around a bit afterwards, with the rescued vessel bobbing merrily in the harbor as backdrop.

But as rewarding as it was—it was also tough, tiring and often frustrating work. Dangerous, too.

Don't forget that Hurricane Marilyn contained an eight to ten foot storm surge. Some unlucky boats ended up ten feet above sea level, *and* a couple of hundred yards away from the water after the storm.

Sometimes it seemed as if we had to refloat the boats on rivers of our own sweat. We'd scream curses at the beached boats, strain against their leaden hulls with damp shoulders, kick cruelly at their scarred keels. "Move, you sum-bitch..." we'd grunt. "Move...!"

"Salvage work is the crude art of refusing to take 'no' for an answer," quipped Big Jack Simmons, one of our merry band of salt-stained Corinthian yacht salvors. "We'd just keep try'n things... yank'n and crank'n and jack'n and wack'n... until the boat either floated or began to *seriously* break apart..."

That sums it up nicely.

Our band of salty St. John salvors was not a formal, well-organized one. It was just a bunch of local boaters who were willing to work long hours doing dangerous work for no pay. Julian Davies, Thatcher Lord, David Dostall, Big Jack Simmons, Ernest Matthias, and Wit Carter were among the men I worked with repeatedly.

It was all totally disorganized. There was no plan. We had no rules. Nobody was a leader. We never discussed things. There was no money involved—we had no roster, schedule, nor official goal.

Thus, we almost always worked effortlessly together as a group.

One of us would want to yank a specific boat back into the water—because we loved the boat or knew the owner or were just tired of seeing it sitting ashore. "Tomorrow after lunch, I'm gonna be out at Maho Bay," one of us would casually mention, "attempting to yank that hard-chimed French ketch back into deep water..."

There was seldom a specific time mentioned. Most members of our gang would not be able to immediately confirm that they'd be there.

(Who'd know what tomorrow might bring?)

But around the appointed time, we'd begin to gather. The vessel owner and the main salvor/friend would usually get there first. They'd formulate a vague plan of attack, just a starting point, really. The rest of us would stumble in over the course of the next couple of hours. (No two 'picks' were ever the same. Improvisation was the name of the game).

We'd bring a mountain of rusty, muddy salvage gear: anchors and rodes and come-alongs and blocks-and-tackles and towlines and lift-bags and air tanks and towboats...

My favorite 'pick' was Richard West's 46 foot wooden ketch *High County*. It was hard aground in Mary's Creek, the harbor directly east of Maho Bay on the island of St. John in the US Virgins.

It was on its port side, with its long bowsprit jutting up well into the mangroves. It was a heavy vessel with a generous lead keel and plenty of wetted surface.

It was not going to be easy getting her off. She drew almost seven feet of water, and she was now resting in about two. Being a carvel-planked wooden vessel, she could not be treated as rudely as a steel, aluminum, or stoutly constructed fiberglass one.

Initial attempts to refloat her had met with total failure. They repeatedly put large anchors out into deep water, and laboriously winched them back to the boat. They had large powerboats surge at heavy towlines without the slightest success.

Richard, her owner/captain, was becoming convinced that *High Country* was going to stay there forever, or at least until some floating crane willing to work on credit took pity on him. (There are, alas, not many such cranes wandering around idle after a major hurricane.)

We showed up, en mass, a few days after the storm.

The first thing we did was lighten up the boat as much as possible. This meant toting numerous heavy objects ashore, as well as emptying her water and fuel tanks, etc.

All the bilge water was removed; the last few drops with a sponge.

A towing bridle of thick nylon rope was carefully wrapped completely around the hull, so that we could pull with confidence. (Without such a bridle, people often get hurt when the fore-bitts or stern cleats get sheared off the deck...

We took a stout halyard, extended it, and ran it ashore to the mangroves. (This would allow us to 'hove down' the hull, and thus lift up the keel once the turn of the bilge was afloat).

In addition, we had a line going from the top of the mizzen mast to a heavy dinghy in the water. This was put into tension, and then, at the appropriate time, six or seven men would clamber into the dinghy, and pump it up and down with body movement. This, too, would 'hove her down.'

Astern of the boat, in the exact path in which we wanted the boat to slide off, we placed our two main 'anchor groups.'

These 'anchor groups' consisted of three or four good-sized anchors closely chained together in a series to reinforce their individual holding power.

Between the anchor groups and the boat was approximately 100 feet of space, filled by six hundred feet of rope roven through a six-to-one block and tackle.... and led to the large cockpit sheet winches on the boat.

In effect, the block and tackles multiplied the power of the sheet winches by six times. Thus, if two robust men cranking the winch handle could exert 2,000 pounds of line pull, the anchor pods would have 12,000 pounds *a piece* pulling on them.

That's a lot of force.

In addition to the two anchor groups, and the 'hove down' lines to the top of each mast—we had two towlines rigged to two large power vessels.

One of these vessels was a large aluminum dive boat with a powerful inboard diesel engine. The other was a somewhat smaller vessel, outboard-powered.

Needless to say, the sandy bottom around the stricken vessel was surveyed carefully, and a path to deep water was selected that contained no rocks, coral heads, or hidden obstructions.

Finally, we were ready to go. A small branch was cut so that it rested exactly on the tip of the bowsprit. (This acted as a reference point to determine movement.)

"Let's take up some slack," said Thatcher Lord, a shipwright from Maine.

Both blocks and tackles had previously been tensioned to the absolute max—and then some. Both tow boats (with bow anchors set) now took a strain, and gradually increased their line pull. The mast head lines were tweaked and pumped as the pulling strains increased.

"Send in the speed boats," someone shouted, as another two small powercraft came buzzing right passed us, throwing the maximum possible wake.

At first nothing happened. No movement. Nothing. The towlines hummed. The blocks creaked. The speed boats made waves. The masts swayed... and nothing.

Nothing.

Then there was a sudden sound, a renting sound, like a large squeaky nail being pried loose from a large wooden board.

"She's moving," shouted Richard excitedly. "She's fucking moving!"

"Cut!" someone shouted, and both tow boats throttled back as we reconsidered.

"Look," said Harold Neel. "We've moved her about a quarter inch, maybe more..."

Nobody was discouraged, just because we had another two hundred feet to go. Any movement, no matter how slight, indicated that we'd eventually get her off—if we just kept trying.

"Let's try it again," said Carolyn Goodlander, "and this time let's see if the speedboats can get even closer with their wakes..."

Four hours later, to a mighty cheer, *High Country* floated off into deep water.

A month after the hurricane, there was still a sunken boat in Cruz Bay. It began to irritate me. By now, our little band of salvors had pretty much disbanded. Most of the boats that could be pulled off or raised up had already been taken care of. Now it was only the derelicts and total wrecks which were left.

Except for that pretty Carl Alberg sloop resting on the bottom of Cruz Bay.

I went to see the owner. He was a local contractor, a nice guy. He'd owned two houses before the storm. He'd lived in one, and rented the other. Now both homes were mere *smears* in the earth. They had been totally flattened by the mini-tornados within Marilyn.

He was wandering around aimlessly with a crowbar amid the wreckage of his life. We talked. He attempted to hide the dampness in his eyes. I was kind enough to pretend I didn't notice.

"As far as the boat goes," he said, and his voice trailed off. "I'd love to see it float again. But I have no time to raise it, nor any money to pay..."

"If I attempt to raise it, and I wrench off the keel or rip off the mast... or I poke a big hole in the side..."

"No liability on your part," he reassured me. "Don't worry about that. You'd be doing me a favor. If you don't refloat it, it will probably just sit there deteriorating, taking up room in the harbor. Sunk, it ain't doing anyone any good..."

I looked at the rubble of his house: water-damaged pictures of his kids fluttering in the air, an open drawer with his wife's undergarmets spilling into the mud, an old sport's trophy which had somehow become decapitated...

I wished I could tie strings to all the corners of his scattered life—and yank them back together again.

But I knew I couldn't.

"I'm not making any promises," I said. "But I'll see what I can do..."

By this point, my wife Carolyn was getting a little weary of salvage work. She'd been with me through most of the rescues, and all the grunting and groaning was beginning to wear thin for her. "It is, alas, hell on my nails," she joked.

Carolyn is quite a women, the light of my life for these past 25 years. She not only can *out work* the average man, she can cook him dinner after.

"Not another one," she begged when I told her of my plan.

"Just one more," I coaxed. "This is the last one, promise. And I really want to do it—seeing that mast sticking up in the middle of the harbor is driving me nuts."

Of course, raising a sunken boat is different from towing one off.

And I didn't have any equipment. Commonsense would indicate that I should not attempt such a complicated job.

But, luckily, commonsense has never been my strong point.

The next day at dawn, I tied my dinghy to the top of the sunken boat's mast. My dinghy was filled with empty plastic milk and water jugs. (Actually, they weren't empty. They were filled with air...)

I dove over the side with my mask and fins and told Carolyn, "Okay! Hand me one..."

I free-dove down to the silent sunken wreck below, opened one of its cockpit lockers, and shoved the air-filled jug within. I repeated the process, again and again and again.

It was easy, mindless work. Surface, breath deep, get a jug, swim down, cram it inside, swim up... surface, breath deep...

When our large dinghy was empty of jugs, I sent Carolyn back to the beach for the cushions and PFDs. Using the same laborious method of transport, I soon had the main cabin of the sunken vessel filled with swim floats, life jackets, and the buoyant cockpit cushions of numerous near-by yachts.

After that, she returned with a dinghy filled with small blocks and large fenders. I dove down, attached the blocks to the toe rails of the boat, and then rove a long line through them. I attached this line to a fender, which also had an 18 inch piece of rope on it.

Then I'd dive back down as Carolyn roared away in the dinghy. When she'd get to the end of the line, the highly buoyant fender would come bubbling down to the block, where it would jam for an instant. During that brief instant while Carolyn was able to keep the strain, I'd tie off the fender to the block and unrove the tow line.

Then we'd do it again.

It was all very low-tech, very slow, very crude. But it worked. Within a couple of hours, the barnacle encrusted boat broke the surface.

By this point, we had help. Wit, Robert, and Frank were swimming alongside us, and they'd brought a couple of small lift bags to make her float even higher.

As soon as she broke the surface, I began towing her towards the beach. It was slow going.

Of course, she ran aground quickly. We paid out a 200 foot long anchor line from her bow through a turning block lashed to a near-by palm tree, and to the fender of my old beat-up jeep.

As I backed up the road (pointing at Ellington's and yet moving towards Wharfside), the boat slid up on the beach on its starboard side as nice as you please.

Now we were able to stand around on the sandy bottom, and jam a bunch of 2x4s under her rail... to keep her upright. Bailing her out was back-breaking, using only a large bucket.

We pulled her off as she floated and soon had her back on her mooring. She was alive again.

It had taken us about ten hours to gather the materials together, and an additional six hours in the water. Cost: zero dollars.

"Isn't she pretty," I said to my wife, pointing at the mud encrusted, barnacled, water-logged mess that she was.

"You're nuts," my wife replied. "Totally nuts! I want to stop this foolishness before you discover the coordinates of the *Titanic*, and tell me to hustle up *fifty billion empty milk jugs...*"

High Country under sail once again

The Last Howl

I am not an anthropologist, but I know that you can tell a lot about a culture by the way they deal with their dead.

On the afternoon of October 22nd, the St. Thomas marine community held *The Last Howl* for live-aboard boater Rick Hagerman. It took place at *Bottom's Up*, the bar/restaurant Rick used to manage at the Independent Boat Yard on the Benner Bay Lagoon.

It was sort of a Caribbean-spiced Irish wake/memorial service, with a decidedly nautical slant. To say it was an 'informal' affair would be to put it mildly. It was about as laid-back and mellow as any thing death-kissed can be.

This was reflected in the quiet mood of the relatively sober crowd. But, despite the solemnness of the occasion, there was still plenty of gentle laughter. People told some outrageous and wild stories about Rick—with a warm 'old shoe' familiarity which said a lot about Rick's easy-going, sun-drenched personality.

Of course, boats are normally the main topic of conversation out there in the anchorage—but it's music which glues this specific harbor community together. Not the kind of *store-bought* music which comes out of a fancy stereo from a hi-tech CD player, but the kind of down-home, toe-tapping folk music which musical friends spontaneously create for friends.

Morgan Whalen played guitar; so did the famous Mighty Whitey. Both of 'em even managed to remember some of the lyrics to the songs they sang, much to the amazement of their regular fans. Dr. Henry Karlin rocked and rolled. Various others salt-stained musicians joined in. Parker Hall and Inflatable Frank took turns plucking on a beat-up washtub bass. Ms. Chris brought down the house with an acappella number. Andrew tapped out some island tunes on his beloved pans.

"Best friend I ever had," said one long-haired, damp-eyed fellow as he stood by the water's edge and faced away from the crowd to hide his chest-quaking emotions. "Rick was.... the best friend I ever had," he repeated softly, looking down into still harbor waters where his red eyes leaked.

Let's get one thing straight—Rick wasn't no 'yachtsman' nor ocean racer nor sea-going yuppie. He was too unpretentious, down-to-earth, bullshitless for that. He was a straight-forward, uncomplicated fellow—a what-you-see-is-what-you-get kinda guy.

His maritime roots stretched all the way back to his native State of Maine. It was there he first went to sea—as a commercial fisherman, not a yachtie.

He'd fish offshore for two or three weeks at a time. This was back in the 1970s. He worked 'before the mast' aboard large steel trawlers. It was a tough life. The storm-tossed waters of the Grand Banks have never been an easy place to eke out a living.

But after a successful fishing trip offshore, Rick would blow back into town with a fistful of money and a powerful thirst. He'd head straight to a ratty little sailor's bar in Booth Bay, Maine. "Let's howl," he'd say with gleeful, heart-felt enthusiasm as he burst through the elbow-battered doors of *McSeagulls*.

And then he'd set about doing just that. *Howl*.

One time, an old downeast fisherman nursing a drink at the dim end of the fist-banged bar said, "Yah. There goes *Mad Dog* Rick again. He likes to *howl*, he does. Strange fellow. Yah..."

Rick would drink and party and wink at women until his well-oiled wallet went belly-up, and then head back out to sea.

He was only about 30 years old, way back in 1980, when he first arrived on St. Thomas. His best buddy, Parker Hall, had invited him down for a brief visit. Rick immediately fell in love with St. Thomas and its rainbow-hued marine community.

He purchased a boat named, appropriately enough, *Rainbow*, and then a Cal 25 named *Ryan's Express*. He settled in. Whatever he was searching for was suddenly all around him.

Sure, Rick loved to party. He could tell a story, relate a joke, or pass on some juicy harbor gossip as well as the next fellow. But there was also a quiet, introspective side to him—as if a lot in life was just a wry joke—and only you and he realized it.

He often communicated in winks, shrugs, and grunts. Sometimes he'd respond perfectly—by not responding at all. He'd roll his eyes, scratch his beard, rub his hands through his hair—and his position on the issue would be crystal clear to friends and foes alike.

Fishing was one of his passions, even when he didn't catch anything. He was one of the original founders of the zany, loony Lagoon Fishing Tournament sponsored by *Bottom's Up*.

These informal fishing tournaments were a lot of fun for everyone, didn't take themselves too seriously, and were an excellent excuse for taking some time off work.

Come to think about it, that sort of sums up Rick too.

Just after midnight, at the height of Hurricane Marilyn, Rick was seen on his foredeck. Or at least a bobbing, weaving flashlight was.

Not long after that, one of his forward anchors let go. When a stern anchor took up, his vessel was caught sideways to the wind and seas for an instant—and under those extreme storm conditions, even a mere instant was far, far too long.

He wasn't a strong swimmer. From the condition of his recovered body, we can only hope it was over quick.

Parker Hall, his best buddy, made the arrangements. Rick was cremated. Forms were filled out, and the appropriate boxes checked off. Mail was canceled. Governmental computer entries were deleted. Such are the modern formalities of death.

Just before sunset, when the Lagoon was bathed in a warm, nostalgic glow from the setting sun, Parker Hall opened up the cardboard box that contained the remains of Rick in a heavy, clear plastic bag.

He reached in, and scattered a handful of fine grey ashes into the Lagoon, a couple of feet from the wobbly barstools of *Bottom's Up*. It wasn't planned, but Parker spontaneously extended the box to someone else, and they too grabbed a handful of Rick and tossed him forlornly into the water. Silently, a solemn line formed. One by one, the hushed crowd filed down to the lapping seashore, and helped scatter Rick into the waters and the shores of his beloved, adopted boating community.

Everyone ended up with grey, ash-stained hands.

"Hey," one of the young boat kids said, tugging at her boatyard-dad's epoxy stained pant's leg. "They're getting some of him in the dinghies! That's not right. Next time he dies, tell 'em *not* to get any of him in the dinghies!"

"Hush, honey," said her mother with a gentle smile.

I stumbled down to the shore in a trance. My feet seemed motorized; strangely disconnected. The air seemed thick and sweet. I could smell the mangroves, earthy and rich with decay.

I took my turn. I said nothing; what was there to say? Just behind me was Kees Stapel, the honorary mayor of nearby Happy Island. Just after he took his turn, he stumbled. I caught him awkwardly in my arms. We both lurched away, grey-handed. His eyes looked wild; his braided beard fiercely snarled in the fading light.

People were hugging each other, leaving grey palm prints on each other's back. Frosty cold beer cans dripped rivulets of grey. In the far corner, a shadowy fellow in a large white Panama hat was rolling up some fat, pungent smokes with grey-stained Zig-zags.

I glanced across the crowd, over to where my wife was talking with Henry Karlin and Morgan Whalen. She had a certain alluring look in her Italian eye, like a young lioness after a feast. She was only a little drunk.

And as I approached, she made a broad, sweeping gesture with her arm—a gesture large enough to encompass not only Rick and his many close friends but all the varied people present... from boat surveyor to boat bum to boat broker to boatbuilder to bilge bunny.

"..family," she was saying, "...he was... these people are... *family!*"

PEOPLE DEM

Joey Borges - Mexico 1968

Joey Borges

When I was a kid I was wild—even more wild than I am now. I liked to show off and do dangerous things; to amaze and startle unsuspecting adults. It was fun. One of my favorite tricks was to ride my bicycle off the dock.

I grew up aboard the 52 foot schooner *Elizabeth*. For years it was docked at Slip #7 Vinoy Basin in St. Petersburg, Florida. Whenever I'd get bored—or a new vessel was pulling into the harbor—I'd do my stunt.

I'd get a couple of blocks away on my bike, and then build up a real head of steam coming back. By the time I'd hit the sidewalk by our dock, I'd be flying flat-out at near super-sonic speeds. I'd lean sharply into the turn, and then straighten up for the last few leg pumps before I'd hit the crude ramp at the end of the dock. The spaces between the dock planks would be vibrating my eyes so roughly that it would be difficult to see. Then suddenly I'd hit the smoothness of the ramp. Soon thereafter... silence as I left the earth, flew over the harbor like a bird, glided over the water like a god...

I'd be screaming at the top of my lungs the whole time, of course, like a demented cross between Peter Pan and Evil Knevil.

Of course, what goes up must come down. Gravity is the one law I've always obeyed. My bike and I would eventually crash into the water with a mighty splash.

I must have been about eight years old at the time—too young to be able to swim it back ashore. So I'd have to leave it on the bottom until evening...

...when my brother-in-law Joey Borges would come home from work. I was only a kid; I didn't know nutt'n about the "in-law" part... I just thought of Joey as my older brother.

"Hey, Joey!" I'd yell as soon as I'd see him. "My bike rolled off the dock again..!"

He'd swear, knowing that a bike does not land a hundred feet away from the end of a dock when it 'falls' off. But he'd always don his mask and fins, and dive it back up for me.

"Don't *do* that anymore," he'd scold me as we'd 3-in-1 oil my upside down bike back to life. "It's too dangerous. One day you're gonna get hurt..."

"OK, Joey," I'd say. "Never again. Did you get the rear axle good?"

"Yeah," he say, "but make sure to lubricate the main sprocket assembly, and those bearing cases between the frame and the pedals..."

Joey was like a God to me—my own personal Atlas. He protected me, taught me, cared for me, watched out for me.

He started out by teaching me how to oil my bike, and then gradually taught me auto, motorcycle, and diesel mechanics. He taught me how to weld, how to use a cutting torch, and how to braze bronze. He taught me when to use a rubber mallet and a soft rag, and when to rely on a Big Sledge and a Large Crowbar to get the job done.

Joey gave me my first motorcycle. It was a Yamaha Twin Jet 100, in three baskets. He helped me put it back together, and even pushed me down the street to get it started. (I learned to ride motorcycles on Joey's old Cushman, and down through the years borrowed a number of his ever-larger bikes...)

He was a man's man. Strong. Virile. Unbeatable. Unshakable.

"Never let 'em see you sweat," he'd whisper to me out of the side of his bearded mouth. He'd always be shifting around a toothpick in his teeth, as if getting ready to decide something of great importance. He'd squint at the horizon, then wink at me. Man-to-man. "Us against the world, kid!" he'd joke. That was Joey.

I still remember him (over thirty years later) in a physical sort of way. He moved as light as a professional dancer—like piano notes floating across a hushed harbor. Despite his gracefulness, he seemed like a giant to me. His arm muscles were huge. He was (in reality) a small, compact, narrow-waisted man, who somehow always seemed bigger than he was. His family was from New Bedford—there were rough New England whalers in his background. Still, my initial boyhood impressions of immense size and strength still persists down through the decades.

The Goodlander family 'adopted' Joey when he was 18 years old, and fresh out of the Navy. He moved aboard our schooner *Elizabeth* in, oh, say, 1959, in Pensacola, Florida.

He quickly adapted to life afloat. You could trust him on the foredeck; sleep soundly when it was his trick at the wheel.

Not long after Joey joined our crew/family/lives, the *Elizabeth* was driven ashore in a gale. It was a pitch black night. Scary. Dangerous.

Joey rowed out the heavy kedges through the breaking surf to prevent the *Elizabeth* from breaking up any further. I watched him through a rain-whipped porthole. He was my hero then, as now. He was swearing at the top of his lungs as he attempted to row out against the breaking seas—and yet never missed an oar stroke. I can still hear my father urging him on. "Put your *back* into it, you FARMER!"

From that storm-tossed night unto eternity... we all loved him.

My sister loved him too. Married him. That made Joey my brother-in-law—on top of being my friend.

Our lives at that point were not perfect.

When we stopped in Carrabelle, Florida, Joey worked as a fisherman on the snapper boats. It was a hard life. He didn't talk about it much. We were poor. (And poverty is never cute.) Joey usually didn't make much money. Fisherman generally don't. But on one trip, his boat got lucky. They found a massive school of snapper off the Campeche Banks of Mexico—that just wouldn't quit. Joey made almost three hundred bucks that trip, and bought a pair of dress shoes.

Joey hadn't had a good pair of shoes in a year. He liked them shoes. He wore his new pair proudly back to the boat. My father spotted Joey and his new shoes. Not realizing that Joey had a pocketful of money for the family fund, my father really lit into him. "How can you buy a pair of store-bought shoes when we're practically starving," he demanded bitterly to Joey. "Are you only thinking of yourself?"

Joey cried. He took off the shoes; never wore them again.

I'll never forget that incident—Joey crying.

Atlas shrugged.

The incident left a deep impression on me—I still can't think about buying a pair of hard shoes without wincing. Such is the randomness of life's lessons.

Later in life, Joey built a 32 foot Friendship sloop in the basement of a funeral home on Cleaver street in Chicago. I helped. Along about the same time, we also built a giant colored egg which we dropped on downtown Chicago at dawn on Easter morning. We made the front page of the Chicago Trib.

Joey had a sense of humor.

Years later, we helped each other build other vessels. I assisted him with the construction of his 42 foot ketch *Rudy B,* and he often helped me with the construction of my 36 foot ketch *Carlotta.*

He loved to encourage people. He was always telling people to "...Go for it!" He was always the spark plug of any group. He liked to motivate, to turn dreams into reality. That's what he was best a—turning ideas into actions. He was a doer. "Hey, whatdaya say we all get together, and help..."

"You can do it!"

"...I believe in you!"

"Don't get discouraged. You're almost there..!"

He loved to teach, to build, to repair—and to see people succeed.

"Plant a tree, build a boat, have a kid," my father told him (and me) many a time.

Joey planted many trees (both literally and figuratively). He built a number of strong boats. He fathered eight children, the youngest of which is currently under two years of age.

And he always liked motorcycles.

A few days ago—on a lonely road, near an empty field, in a sad New England town—Joey had a stroke while astride his beloved steel steed. He was doing hull-speed at the time. He sailed into a tree, and eternity.

When I heard the news, all I could think about was gathering all the shattered pieces of the accident back together again, and sprinkling them with 3-in-1 oil, and whispering, "Don't *do* that anymore, Joey. It's too dangerous..."

But that's absurd. And I will resist the temptation to be angry with God for taking him, and instead be thankful to God for having sent him.

Everyone needs a big brother. I was fortunate enough to have one. At least for awhile.

Joey Borges - Florida early 1960's

Piercing Waves and Fallacies
...the story of Roger Hatfield & The Gold Coast Boys...

Roger Hatfield owes much of his current success to his notoriously weak stomach. It is not something the reclusive naval architect who founded Gold Coast Yachts of St. Croix likes to admit... but the fact is Hatfield gets seasick almost every time he goes offshore. And we're not talking about getting a little *queasy* either— we're talking about 'somebody-shoot-me-I-want-to-die' seasick. Topsides, Hatfield's standard racing position is at the loo'ard rail. Belowdecks, he hangs out in the head while "calling his ole friend 'Ralph!' on the big white phone."

"Yeah," says a close friend of Hatfield's who has sailed many an ocean mile with him, "Roger pukes like a metronome in heavy weather!"

When pressed, Hatfield shyly admits, "I've spent a lot of time at sea on various sailing craft—wishing I was dead. Being sick is no fun. I can sort of laugh about it later, but not at the time. Most sailing monohulls have a very nauseating motion, especially compared to multihulls. Monohulls have a sickeningly slow lurch to leeward, and then a drunken roll back up to windward—all combined with that stomach-flopping pitching motion. Monohull powercraft are often even worse. The constant pounding of a modern planing hull is horrible even in a moderate sea..."

Despite the sensitivity of Hatfield's inner ear and his easily disturbed stomach, he spends a lot of his time sailing and racing aboard his multihull designs. In addition, he lives on an island in the middle of the Caribbean Sea, and thus is constantly riding on various inter-island ferries.

"The result of all this self-induced suffering," says Hatfield, "is that I have done a tremendous amount of thinking about the subject of passenger comfort. Yes, I want my commercial passenger carrying multihulls to be as fast, safe, economical, profitable, and practical as possible—but I also want them to be comfortable too. To me, passenger comfort is a key element of any successful design."

Hatfield, a 44 year old lanky fellow who was originally born in Maryland, now lives in an area which is an ideal testing ground for such designs. The local Nor'east tradewinds seldom stop blowing in St. Croix, and often pipe up to 25 knots for weeks at a time. Sea conditions are often quite rough, with three to five foot waves the norm.

So a couple of years back, Roger Hatfield began considering exactly what it would take to design and build the smoothest riding, safest, most economical small passenger ferry in the world.

Needless to say, there was some initial resistance to the idea among his many friends and co-workers. After all, this was a radical design departure for Hatfield. He and his merry band of tropical wood-gluers at Gold Coast Yachts had established their worldwide reputation by custom- building over 30 large, USCG approved, passenger daysailing catamarans—not power-driven ferry boats.

A major part of the success of the company was directly related to the *profitability* of their sailing catamarans. They weren't just building hulls—they were also building floating money machines.

Eventually, the word got out internationally—if you wanted a sailing 'cash cow', then you ordered a 'cattle-maran' from Gold Coast.

And now just—when things where going so damn good and their daysail boats were back-ordered almost a year in advance—Hatfield was announcing that he was going to build a small multihull *powerboat,* and that it wasn't going to *float* on top of the water but rather *drive through* the tops of the waves...

What precipitated such corporate madness?

It all began in the late 1970s, when a young, starry-eyed, long-haired kid named Roger Hatfield sailed into St. Croix aboard his 31 foot *Sea Runner* trimaran. Back in those days, the island of St. Croix was *the* Caribbean mecca for multihullers. Dick Newick and Peter Spronk were both familiar faces at the shipyard glue-pots and shoreside rum shops of Christiansted.

Strange and wondrous boats were constantly being built everywhere on the island. There was an almost physical synergy crackling in the air. Everyone shared their building techniques, bragged about their successes, and wailed about their failures. Designing and building multihulls on St. Croix wasn't just a hobby or a profession back then—it was an exciting life-style which bordered on religion.

To young, impressionable Roger Hatfield, the son of a staid MIT naval architect, it was all pretty heady stuff.

"Everybody's learning curve was pretty steep," remembers Hatfield. "I learned a hell of a lot from Dick Newick and Peter Spronk. By that time, of course, I was totally in awe of Jim Brown—I mean, he was literally my hero, my multihull guru. After awhile, I came in contact with Jan and Meade Gougeon up in Bay City, Michigan. It seemed as if great ideas and clever ways of building things were just exploding all around me..."

Hatfield started doing minor repairs on some local boats to earn some pocket change. Word of his remarkable ability as a 'wood butcher' soon spread, and he was quickly flooded with complicated repair jobs. The quality of his work was soon noticed by a local entrepreneur and business executive named Richard Difede, a fellow whom Hatfield had known slightly back in the States. Difede immediately recognized Hatfield's undeniable talent as a shipwright—but also picked up his obvious lack of business savvy. It seemed a shame to Difede that Hatfield had all that talent and all those willing customers—but not the business sense to put them together in a meaningful, profitable way.

"Perhaps," Difede thought idly, "with a little organizational help from me..."

Despite having vastly different personalities—or perhaps because of it—the two men immediately hit it off as business partners.

"Richard is the business brains behind Gold Coast," says Hatfield. "If it wasn't for him, I'd still be fixing up 'mashed-up' boats under a shady palm tree..."

The first boat they built was for a local fellow named Heinz Punzenburger. It was a 42 foot trimaran named *Terero*, and was an immediate success.

Ten years down the road—and many happy passengers and profitable dollars later—it is *still* in daily service along the rough north coast of St. Croix.

"Of course," said Hatfield, "back then my emotional commitment was to trimarans. I'd built two of them previously, and was convinced that they were slightly faster, better-handling, and more maneuverable than catamarans."

"But I'm a practical, realistic sort of guy, and I could see the design and construction advantages of a large catamaran. Let's face it; they are a lot simpler. They have fewer parts and are cheaper to build. In addition, your average daysail customer seems intrinsically more comfortable with two hulls than three."

"So I started thinking... how could I end up with an economical multihull that combined the simplicity of a cat with the sailing performance and handling characteristics of a tri?"

There was some resistance to this tri-to-cat notion within the local multihull community.

"I was amazed," said Hatfield. "It was kind of like a religious question. The whole tri-versus-cat debate can get very heated. Some multihull people worship catamarans and others worship tris and never the twain shall meet!"

Despite this, Hatfield's next boat was a fifty-some foot catamaran named *Nube Volante* ('Flying Cloud' in Spanish). By using deep, fat foils, a high aspect rig, and a rounded hull shape—Hatfield was able to build a practical, inexpensive catamaran that handled *almost* as good as a more complicated and expensive trimaran.

"Dick Newick used to advise me to divide up my professional life into three parts; playing on boats, working in the shop, and designing. Dick's idea was that if you didn't play around with boats a whole bunch and deal with the nitty-gritty of building them—then you could never really become an insightful designer. I think there is some truth to that. Anyone who seriously wants to play the game should spend some time paddling around in a canoe..."

Hatfield constantly 'tweaked' his designs. Instead of making them more complicated, he made them simpler, stronger, lighter, and more easily maintained.

With his boats continuously carrying thousands of paying passengers per week under very stressful sea conditions, Gold Coast Yachts was in a unique position to refine its products.

Hatfield continuously networked with his vessel's owners and their captains. How could he design the boat to be safer? Was there anything that could be changed to make it easier to clean-up and hose-down after a charter? What made noise, and how could he silence it? Were the sheet winches positioned well, and the line stoppers convenient to use? What about the..?

The result was a growing reputation for dependable boats that *worked* day after day after day.

Orders poured in. The word got out that Hatfield was the new 'guru of glue' on St. Croix, and some of the most sought-after shipwrights in the Caribbean made the pilgrimage to Salt River to work with the notoriously hard-working, highly-innovative, multi-ethnic 'Zebra Crew' of Gold Coast.

It wasn't long before there were 25 employees, and they were popping out another finished 'turn-key' USCG approved multi-passenger vessel every three months.

Their most successful design was a 53 foot catamaran with a rotating wing-mast that could carry 49 passengers in comfort and safety—while still occasionally hitting speeds of 20 knots.

It was a no nonsense, utterly practical design which featured a truly mammoth cockpit and huge food/entertainment pod.

The hulls were made out of strip-planked cedar which was covered with uniglass both inside and out. The materials were basically low-tech—the elegance was in the low-maintenance structural design which incorporated numerous cored panels and plywood box beams.

Passenger safety was a major consideration—the steering station and all the sail control systems were totally separate from the passenger area.

Despite its massive cockpit and deck area, the boat was still thrilling to sail and responsive to handle. It easily tacked from broad reach to broad reach—a trick many large cats find difficult.

To spice things up, Gold Coast also built a few 'special order' yachts based on their commercial designs. In addition, Hatfield whipped up a flat-out racing trimaran named *Hatter* which he successfully sailed into the winner's circle at most of the major multihull regattas in the Caribbean.

One of his first forays into heavily powered multihulls was a 55 foot 'fast motorsailer' catamaran that was powered by two Cummins 220hp diesels in addition to its large wingmast. On its maiden voyage to Hawaii *The Spirit of Kauai* averaged a respectable 11.5 knots under sail. There is nothing too astounding about such a speed in a modern multihull—but what is astounding is that it occasionally zoomed along at over 24 knots under sail and at 24 knots *under power alone*. And this isn't some exotic, high-tech carbon-fiber, super expensive ocean racer, it is a USCG approved 49 foot passenger *money machine* which can easily run through big surf inlets, anchor almost right on the beach, and never heel over far enough to scare the meekest of landlubbing tourists. Now *that's* truly remarkable!

"One of the design features I gave a lot of consideration to was the shape of the bows of my catamarans," said Hatfield. "If a knowledgeable racing sailor pushes a correctly-designed racing catamaran beyond her limits, he should be able to sense that she might go over, but not necessarily if she is going to pitch-pole or broach. If she is correctly designed, she will be on the verge of both when pressed beyond her limits..."

"...but part of the reason for this is because her 'engine'—her mast and rigging and sails—is literally up in the air. So I asked myself what a 'soft' riding catamaran hull should look like if its engine wasn't 'aloft' but aft at the waterline.

"It was immediately obvious to me that the bows of a smooth riding power cat should be much narrower and less buoyant than a sail-driven vessel, and this quickly led me to consider the idea of a wave piercer..."

A wave piercer catamaran is a boat with two long, needle-like, low buoyancy, 'weakly hunting' hulls which slice cleanly through the waves without being forced to immediately contour to them. This greatly reduces slamming and pounding. The passenger 'box' flies above these arrow-like hulls, and sits well aft.

"The reason that wave piercers are so comfortable," said Hatfield, "is because by the time the wave crest gets directly under the forward edge of the bridge deck—the vessel has just begun to gently lift itself up to allow the wave to pass underneath it. There is relatively little pitching motion.

"We humans have already adjusted somewhat to vertical accelerations—most of us walk, ride in cars, and fly on airplanes without much motion sickness. That's not the problem. It's the pitching and rolling motions which get to us..."

The Australians were the original pioneers of the wave piercing concept. They built a 300 passenger, 91 foot model back in 1985. It featured relatively short, narrow, deep-V hulls with flat decks.

In many ways it was an immediate success. There is no question that it provided an amazingly smooth ride. Passenger satisfaction was extremely high. However, running downwind in a major gale—it once 'stuffed' its two bows. A few of the passengers suffered minor injuries, and the concept got a black eye.

"The reason it stuffed its bows was two-fold," said Hatfield. "One reason was because the hulls weren't nearly as long and far forward as they needed to be. The other reason was because of those flat decks. Once they dove underwater at high speed, they were forced under even deeper."

To Hatfield, the solution was easy and apparent: make the hulls as long and narrow as practical, and design the hulls to easily move *vertically* through the water.

"Of course we want the hulls of a wave piercer to drop into the water quickly on the downstroke," said Hatfield, "but we also want them to *rise* easily too. That's the key."

The more Hatfield explored the idea of a wave piercer with low buoyancy hulls designed for *minimum vertical resistance*—the more the idea made sense to him. (Hatfield now holds a patent on two of the most important aspects of his wave piercing design.)

He went to his drawing board, and drew design after design. With each new refinement, he got closer to his 'ideal' wave piercer.

He eventually settled on five basic criteria: safety, passenger comfort, speed, ease of maintenance, and profitability.

Safety was at the top of his list—as it is with any moral designer of passenger craft. Hatfield felt his wave piercing concept had some significant advantages in this area.

The main one was positive flotation. Most commercial ferry boats will sink if holed. Hatfield's wave piercers will not. Its hulls are divided up into separate watertight compartments. If one compartment becomes flooded, the boat should still be able to proceed to port under its own power. Even if a couple of the compartments were flooded, it would not sink. In essence, the boat is its own liferaft. To Hatfield, this is a significant and valuable feature.

Fuel economy is always a factor in any commercial design. Displacement hulls (like supertankers) are very cost-efficient ways to move heavy cargo slowly. But people are relatively low-density cargo, and they like to move fast. Planing hulls (like sportfishing boats) are efficient at high speeds; but they can only maintain those high speeds in calm water without massive passenger discomfort.

Only a wave piercer can quickly move a good number of people through fairly rough seas without a massive amount of passenger discomfort—and are able to do so with a remarkable amount of fuel efficiency.

This brings us to the subject of maintenance. We all know boats require a relatively high degree of maintenance because of their corrosive salt-water environment. This is unavoidable.

But, in comparison with other types of ferries, wave piercers are simple, uncomplicated mechanical devices. They are easily driven, and thus their engines can be smaller and simpler than other craft. Hovercraft are extremely complicated; too complicated to even quickly describe. Hydrofoils require a massive amount of horsepower. Both are noisy fuel guzzlers. Only the wave piercers provide good speed with passenger comfort in moderate seas with quiet fuel efficiency.

Speed is, of course, another consideration. People who want to spend a day on a nearby island don't want to spend half a day getting there and half a day getting back.

But the top speed of a transportation system is only one aspect of *how long it takes to get there*. Airplanes are very fast; but getting your luggage, a taxi, and arriving at your final destination often negates their speed advantage. Ferries can often get their passengers closer to their final destination—a big plus. Wave piercers are even more advantageous because they can maintain high speeds without sizable wakes in close quarters. When other ferries must throttle back, wave piercers can just 'keep on trucking' without disturbing other vessels in the harbor or eroding its shoreline.

The last factor is, of course, passenger comfort. This is where a wave piercer really shines. Its narrow, 'weakly hunting' needle hulls slice through the tops of large waves without slamming into them, diving under them, or bashing on top of them.

The result is a fairly smooth 'turbo-ride' neither totally in the water nor on top of it —but rather straddling its frothy surface.

Of course, in extreme conditions, these craft are not immune to motion. People can, and do, get sick on occasion. But motion studies have shown that far less people feel ill on a wave piercer in larger seas at higher speeds than almost any other type of passenger craft.

No matter how Hatfield played with the numbers and viewed the research data —wave piercers came out on top. He felt he was really onto something, but he also knew he had to 'show not tell'. Professional seafarers are a notoriously conservative lot. This wasn't like talking a trimaran sailor into considering a catamaran; a wave piercer was a totally different species of animal.

So Hatfield went in search of the perfect customer, and soon came up with a fellow named Per Dohm.

Dohm qualified on a number of fronts. He was a knowledgeable seaman. He owned and operated a profitable local 'water taxi' service. He was pro-multihull.

The only problem was that his current multihull ferry was practically brand new —and a severe disappointment. It had fallen far short of his original expectations.

"I run between St. Thomas and St. John across Pillsbury Sound dozens of times every day," said Dohm in a recent interview. "It isn't a long run, but it can be rough —especially when the wind opposes the current. Under those conditions, the seas get all humped up and confused. With my other boat, I had to slow down to a crawl..."

Hatfield set out to sell Per Dohm a wave piercer. It wasn't easy. Dohn didn't want to make another mistake, especially so soon after his previous multihull fiasco. It took time, patience, and cunning. But Hatfield can be an effective salesman. He passionately believes in his product, and is totally committed to design innovation.

Hatfield sold Dohm on the concept of a wave piercer with two main arguments. One, it would seldom have to throttle back because of the steep waves. Two, it could travel deeper into the anchorages at higher speeds because the design would create almost no wake.

The result was *Galileo,* a 40 foot wave piercer powered by twin 200hp Yamaha outboards. It is USCG licensed to carry 24 passengers.

"After so many years of thinking about it," said Hatfield, "it was a real thrill to finally sea trial the actual boat. I had high hopes, but the smoothness of the ride exceeded them. The sensation of a well-designed wave piercer traveling at speed in a moderate sea... is a totally unique experience. There's nothing quite like it. It is something which almost has to be experienced to be believed."

"At first it felt very strange to me to be propelled that fast through the water without being stopped or hammered by the waves," recalled Hatfield. "We'd come rushing straight at a big wave, and I'd instinctively brace myself for the crash—but it just wouldn't be there. I just kept saying, 'Wow!' and 'Gee!' and 'Gosh!' like I was a little kid with his first two-wheel bike. The thing that struck me at the very outset was how much *fun* these boats were!"

Did Per Dohm like it? You could say so; within a year, he'd purchased a second wave piercer from Gold Coast. "I like them. But that's not the important thing," said Dohm. "My passengers like 'em. *That's* the important thing!"

When the prestigious Little Dix Bay Resort needed a small ferry on an emergency basis, Dohm temporarily leased them his first wave piercer for a couple of months. It smoothed out the Tortola to Virgin Gorda run so well that Little Dix ordered a new one for itself, as did a couple of the local dive shops.

The boats literally sold themselves. As soon as a new one was put in service at a new location, Gold Coast Yachts would be hit with a new batch of orders. Hatfield explains it this way. "They work, they're practical, and they're fun. People like fun boats—even the most jaded professionals want something that is interesting to drive..."

His next challenge was a considerably bigger design. A company on Sint Maarten wanted an economical ferry that could carry 50 people at 24 knots across the open ocean between Saba, St. Barts, and Sint Maarten—and could do so with some reasonable level of passenger comfort.

In many ways it was the ultimate test, a 'put up or shut up' challenge to Hatfield. He signed a tightly worded contract specifying exactly how fast the boat would have to go while carrying what payload through what sea conditions. If the boat didn't meet or exceed them, Hatfield & Company would have to 'eat the boat'.

This effectively put his entire company at risk. "Sure, I was confident..." gulped Hatfield.

The result was *The Edge*, a sixty foot, 50 passenger wave piercer. It weighed 31,000 pounds, was powered by twin 425hp Lugger engines coupled to two Hamilton jetdrives, and only burned 28 gallons an hour.

She passed her sea trials with ease, and her owners reported three months after her first run that she hadn't missed a single day of service because of sea conditions or mechanical problems.

Next on the drawing board—scheduled for construction in late 1995—is a 104 foot wave piercer intended for passenger service between St. Croix and St. Thomas. It will seat 125 passengers, be air-conditioned, and have a top speed of 35 knots. It is expected to make eight daily trips across the 40 mile stretch of open sea. It will be powered by four diesels, so that it can keep to its schedule with any single engine down for maintenance.

The only problem Hatfield foresees is an aesthetic one.

"The appearance of these boats strike some people as rather odd," admits Hatfield. "I too, at first, found them strange to look at. But they grow on you. Form ultimately follows function. Today we marvel at the perfect proportions of a flying glider; yesterday we scoffed at the ugliness of the Wright Brothers original effort..."

Are Roger Hatfield and his Gold Coast yachts on the leading edge of a revolution in small passenger craft? Can his forty and sixty footers be scaled up to a hundred feet and beyond? Are these new 'patented' wave piercers a true breakthrough—or just another semi-smooth bump along the design road?

Only time will tell.

But one thing is clear. It won't take *much* time. The world is watching. Ferries like *The Edge* are regularly being checked out by sharp-eyed men in expensive business suits who have engineering calculators in their hands and dollar signs in their eyes. If this second batch of wave piercers are as economical, profitable and comfortable as the first—then the world will be beating a path to the door of Roger Hatfield and Gold Coast Yachts.

Virgin Fire is a fine example of a custom multihull
built by Gold Coast Yachts.

Steveo

This spring Steveo-The-Monkey decided he'd either been in the islands too long... or not long enough. To discover which, he went to New England for the summer.

Now Steveo had been living on St. John for many years. He worked construction all week, and races sailboats in his spare time. Nice life. When he got to Newport, things seemed ideal. There was lots of work and a million racing boats. "Just the place for me," said Steveo. He approached the first stranger on the street he spotted wearing deckshoes, and said, "Hey, you! Where's the nearest sailor's bar?"

Steveo was soon belly up to a waterfront bar filled with racing sailors—and having a swell time. Sea stories filled the air, and with Steveo telling his wild tales of Caribbean ocean racing—he soon had a crowd around him. Everything was going great until somebody asked him, "I say, Old Boy! That does sound rather exciting! I'm in banking... what do you do for a living?"

"I pound nails," grinned Steveo. "Construction. Whatever."

And the crowd suddenly drew back as if smelling an offensive odor. "Construction..?" somebody muttered in the same tone of voice Nancy Reagan might say the word 'child molester'... "how... how... quaint!"

"I'm afraid you've got the wrong bar..." another said to Steveo. "Tradesmen drink down the street a ways..."

Now Steveo knows when he's not wanted. So he stumbled out of the sailor's bar, approached the first rough looking dude on the street wearing cement stained boots, and said, "Hey, you! Where's the nearest bar where construction workers hang out?"

Steveo was soon belly-up to another bar with a slightly more boisterous crowd. Guys with ripped leather nail pouches, tape measurers, and hammers hanging from their belts filled the joint. He quickly made a few friends, and became engrossed in conversation about banging nails in the Caribbean... until one of the guys slapped him on the back hard enough to kill a horse, and asked, "Whatta you do fer *fun*? Huh? How do ya get yer rocks off?"

"Oh," said Steveo, "...I kind of like to race sailboats..."

And the crowd of construction workers drew back as if they'd just detected Steveo was wearing Chanel No 5. "You a fairy?" somebody asked with a burp. "Wrong Bar!" somebody shouted in back...

So Steveo is back on St. John now—banging nails all day and sailing/racing as often as possible. After work, he often drops into the Back Yard Bar on St. John for a beer. Nearly everyone there is either working construction, sailing, racing, chartering or doing some strange

& twisted combination of all four.

   Oh yeah. Steveo's on the look-out for someone from Newport. He's going to buy the guy a drink—and make sure nobody says "Wrong bar!" to him.

Steveo was an integral member of the infamous "Monkey Crew"
of the racing yacht *Stormy Weather*.

Fritz Seyfarth: Caribbean Sea Gypsy

Twenty-five years ago—just as this publication (author's note: this piece originally appeared in Sailing magazine) was being launched—another literary voyage commenced. A shy petroleum engineer from Texas named Fritz Seyfarth waited outside his boss's office to be congratulated. His recent oil-well field report had been a masterpiece of prose. It really *sang!*

"Enter!" barked the door, Fritz did, and the large man with the cigar behind the polished desk exploded... "Don't you EVER submit a report to me like this again! It reads like a... a.... Soap Opera...!"

Fritz's jawed dropped in amazement. Then his one good eye (he's blind in his left) unfocused for a second, and the room seemed to dissolve. He was at sea aboard his beloved ketch *Tumbleweed*. They were beam reaching in the tropics—perfect trade wind conditions. He could hear the gentle creak of her stout bulkheads, watch her bow dip & curtsy to the waves, smell that tangy salt air....

"And so," concluded his boss, yanking Fritz back to reality, "never vary from the accepted form again!"

"I won't," Fritz said quietly. "I quit."

Tumbleweed is a 40 foot John Alden wooden (cedar on oak) ketch built by Schaetzel Boat Yacht in 1935. When Fritz first looked at her tethered forlornly to a dock in San Diego, he considered her too old, too beat up, and too expensive to buy. Then he went below. There was something about her... he could sense a sea-kindly soul. He rested his head upon a faded pillow. It was so peaceful and safe inside her belly. Whether he was sleeping or just daydreaming he's not sure; "Take me, Fritz," her soft voice whispered into his ear, "*Please* take me!"

The moment was a pivotal one—both their lives were forever changed. After nearly three decades and 100,000 ocean miles, the love affair continues. Fritz is not jaded, not tired of his life as a restless sea gypsy, not ready yet to 'come to his senses.' The boat is still eager to point her bowsprit towards a distant horizon.

"Someday I may decide to 'swallow the hook' and move ashore," admits Fritz, "but not soon. I'm having too much fun knocking about the Caribbean. There's still a lot of ocean out there; a lot of islands I've never visited. I'm not the least bit bored. This is as close to paradise as I'll ever get on earth. As a matter of fact, as soon as I finish up some woodwork on the cockpit sole..."

Fritz has sailed to Hawaii, Tahiti, and Mexico. He has cruised the west, south, and east coasts of North America. He's seen most of

Central America, and the north coast of South America. He's been to nearly every tropical isle in the Caribbean. He once pulled into Panama with "... twenty cents, American." For over twenty five years now, he has sailed wherever wind and whim push. He has lived a life of rare adventure and freedom most men only dream. Ten thousand sunsets, a million friends, and enough memories for a dozen lifetimes have bobbed in his wake.

"You can still do it," he claims. "It is no more difficult today than it was yesterday. The Dream is still possible. There is still plenty of sea-room in Paradise for a sea gypsy. I've never regretted casting off my docklines, and unshackling myself from so-called civilization."

It is difficult for his fellow sea-rovers to remember that Fritz is now 64 years old. He seems so boyish.—he moves upon the deck of *Tumbleweed* like a spry teenager. He often single-hands into an anchorage under full sail. As the boat slows head-to-wind, he leisurely strolls forward. His left hand nonchalantly releases the main halyard as he passes by, and soon he's clapped a couple of lashings on the jib. A barefoot toe tips over the rusty, over-sized anchor. The boat is soon secure, shipshape, and ever-ready to go back to sea.

Fritz seems to have—after a lifetime at sea—discovered the Fountain of Youth not as a destination but as a journey. Both man and boat keep getting simpler; the boat's auxiliary engine was deep-sixed, his Plath sextant was replaced with a plastic one, the cabin lights gradually evolved into kerosene.

"There's not too much I need anymore," says Fritz, "not too much I want. Although I don't make much money, I make more than I spend. A good compass, an accurate clock... what else is there, really?"

Perhaps the key to Fritz's personality is Texas. He grew up on a ranch. He's really just an ole intellectual cowpoke who has traded in his horse for a boat. 'Don't Tread On Me' could be his private yacht ensign. While attending Texas A&M, working with the famous oil rig firefighter Red Adair, or moonlighting as an oceanographer at the Scripp's Institute—Fritz amused himself riding bulls at the rodeo. "I guess I wasn't too good," he says ruefully. "I broke my arms seven times. The last time I rode, the bull busted both of 'em, and then trampled me for good measure. I finally got the message. Going to sea seemed awful easy after that..."

Fritz's dream wasn't just to sail into the sunset. His dream was also to write his way across the oceans—to be a salt-stained, sea-going inkslinger. He sold his first story ("Race that Cruising Clunker!") to a local 'fishwrapper' marine newspaper. He was in ecstasy—and so what if he'd gotten paid $60, and had $75 invested in the photos?

He became a full-time professional freelancer. His book "Tales of the Caribbean" was well received, and he soon formed *Spanish Main*

Press to publish "Mavericks in Paradise," "The Sea Gypsies Handbook," and numerous other marine-related books.

With the six or seven professional yacht deliveries he does each year, the occasion charter, and his writing income—he's wealthy by his own modest standards. "I was thinking about being a teacher because I'd get the summer off, and every seven years I could take a sabbatical. I liked the ratio, but figured they had it backwards. I prefer seven year sabbaticals, and then a year of work..." He thinks about it for a moment. "Maybe less..."

Of course, Fritz—like most men of the sea—has a selective memory. He only recalls the good times. All the wet, cold, miserable gales are quickly forgotten. He can feel fear; he just can't remember it. He is equally kind to his boat—his eye observes only her best qualities.

But all of his sailing hasn't been without mishap. In the mid 70's, while single-handing about 350 miles Nor'west of Puerto Rico towards the Lesser Antilles, Fritz and *Tumbleweed* were struck by a large freighter. It stopped, looked, and left.

Tumbleweed's mainmast was snapped in two, and the hull was leaking badly. Fritz hoisted himself aloft to save what was left of the mast. The boat was rolling wildly. It was worse than any bull he'd ever rode. He was at spreader level when something broke, and he fell to the deck. The pain was intense. He could barely move. He blacked out/in/out. Time went by. Finally, he was able to crawl below, and begin pumping.

It got dark, and really started to blow. What was left of both masts went over the side. Occasionally, he'd stop pumping long enough to quickly stuff a life jacket, fender, or seat cushion into some of the holes in the topsides. It was the longest night of his life.

At dawn, he cut away his mainmast rigging which had been attempting to sink the boat all night. The boat shot off to loo'ard, and the mast appeared to sail to windward, waving a broken spreader in triumphant good-bye. "So long, you reaching fool," it seemed to say to Fritz. "I tried for years to make you go to weather, but you just would never learn!"

Fritz smiled—alone in an empty sea—but only for a moment. The situation was serious. He'd transmitted a MAYDAY on his radio, and received no reply. Three long days and three long nights went by. The water was now leaking into *Tumbleweed* faster than he could pump it out. He was getting tired—so very tired. He started to think he might not make it. *Tumbleweed* was going down. He put some emergency food in his eight foot sailing pram. The two hundred mile storm-tossed passage to the nearest island was going to be a rather sporty proposition...

Just as the last of his strength was ebbing away—just at dusk—a

Coast Guard vessel appeared out of the gloom. Later, he'd learned it had heard his weak MAYDAY. As it swung alongside, and prepared to launch its boats to bring him pumps—Fritz couldn't believe its name: USCG Cutter *Sagebrush* had come to rescue *Tumbleweed*.

It seemed somehow rather fitting—at least to a Texas cowboy turned sea gypsy named Fritz Seyfarth.

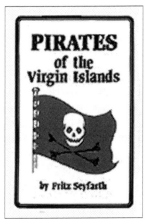

Fritz has recently died,
but his books live on.

Captain John Smith
The Man, The Myth, and the Madness of the
MERMAID OF CARRIACOU

The *Mermaid of Carriacou* is certainly the most famous 'island sloop' currently afloat in the Lesser Antilles. She's a special boat—a happy, blessed boat. Exactly why this particular beach-built wooden vessel is so remarkable is difficult to say: yet easily felt once aboard her worn, rough-hewn decks. Her planks—her very bones!— seem to radiate a sense of freedom, contentment, and rare possibility. She has a warm, friendly heart. To sail her is to love her.

Since 1968 this has been true; and sailors throughout the Caribbean have sensed it. (Author's Note: True, some unfortunate people can not feel the strong heartbeat of a good ship—nor feel the agony of her death throes upon a storm-tossed reef—but this article isn't written for them. Instead, it is penned for people who can sometimes feel what they cannot accurately measure. I, personally, am not sure there is a God in Heaven—yet I'm certain the *Mermaid of Carriacou* has a soul.)

Mermaid of Carriacou was built by Zepharin MacLaren at Windward, Carriacou, for American yachtsman and adventurer J. Lynton Rigg. She is 44 feet long with 13 feet of beam, and has a moderate draft. She is somewhat slabsided—with sharp floors, extreme deadrise, and a graceful entry. She has a long straight run aft. The design—especially when loaded with cargo and heeled by the Trades—is a sweet one.

Rigg's idea was to build a fast 'island sloop,' and challenge all the local native boat-builders to a race for a sizable amount of money ($500EC). Rigg's motivation was not merely to win—but to foster and rekindle the dying art of shipbuilding which had been a flourishing business on the island until the early 1960s.

His simple yet clever plan was a success—a huge success. He had *Mermaid* built, and organized the Carriacou Regatta. His vessel easily walked away with 1st Place, and all the local builder's vowed, "Never again!"

Numerous vessels were built to beat her—none did for many years. (It is rumored she won eight or nine Carriacou regattas before she started getting beat by 'cargo' boats with 2 inch deck beams: her's are eight inches by eight inches!)

Yet—in a sense—all of her varied challengers were winners. Shipbuilding on the tiny, dry, unimportant island of Carriacou grew into a respected profession. Soon Carriacou boats were sailing up and down the Lesser Antilles again—making a new name for themselves. People had work; people had pride. They used their boatbuilding skills and their knowledge of the sea to carve out a decent living on an otherwise dirt-poor rock.

An entire island got a new lease on life—and a new deserved reason for self-respect.

Perhaps that's why *Mermaid of Carriacou* has such a benign, welcoming spirit. Perhaps she carries some of the joyful pride of the many-hued peoples of Carriacou locked deep within her oaken heart.

Of course, such a strange and wonderful vessel deserves an extraordinary owner/captain. Someone who is willing to devote his entire life to maintaining her rightful place in Caribe history. Someone dumb enough to want to; smart enough to succeed. A wonderful, care-free fool of enormous proportions.

Enter the notorious, the infamous, the scandalous, the improbable, the impossible, the outrageous Captain John Smith. It was fate: such a famous boat with such a rich past *needed* a strong skipper and *Mermaid of Carriacou* found one in Smith.

He is.... John Smith is... hard to explain.

He is a poet, a sailor, a writer, a rummy, an axe & sledgehammer shipwright, an optimist, a sailmaker, an explorer, a 10 cent Philosopher, a madman, a Yankee Trader, an honest con-man, a visionary, a genius, and a Complete and Utter Fool.

Luckily, he has a parrot named Bianca who does most of his long-range thinking and offshore navigation. The bird's got a quick brain; too bad its foul mouth and disgustingly graphic sexual suggestions prevent it from interacting much with civilization.

John Smith is sort of like an Indiana Jones who got a little too twisted during the 1960's—and actually believed all that crap about peace, love, brotherhood, and the Rights of Man.

In 1977, he heard that the *Mermaid* was for sale cheap—because she was built without an engine, was too big to fish, and too small to carry freight.

Smith rushed down-island—waving a fistful of Yankee Greenbacks, and proudly purchased her from the amazed, amused sailors of Carriacou.

Many knowledgeable folks attempted to dissuade John from the purchase. One well-known USVI yachtsman said bluntly, "That boat ain't just leak'n, John—she's sinking! She ain't worth trying to bring back to life! Attempting to fix her up would be like putting perfume on a pig..!"

Needless to say, John ignored the skeptics.

He paid his money, took his chance, and has never regretted his decision.

Thus, he gradually began to be known throughout the Caribbean as

"De white mon wid de black mon's boat!"

He's sailed from Maine to South America—and carried inter-island cargos of fruits and trees and lumber and salt and anything/everything which would pay.

He regularly charters his vessel for $20.00 per day per person. (When Smith says no-frills—he means it! If you wanna glass of water; bring one.)

Captain John Smith doesn't go by the Rule Book. In fact, he ate his copy. Or he ate the cockroaches who ate it. Whatever. Just 'cause some idiot makes a rule, doesn't mean you should obey it, according to Smith. He's been repeatedly arrested for having too much fun, detained for not being serious enough, and stomped nearly to death by some violence-crazed Grenadian Gairy goons who thought he was acting 'far too free to be allowed to flee...'

He was a strong supporter of Maurice Bishop of Grenada when Mr. Bishop was alive—and Smith still passionately believes in weird, untrendy causes like truth, justice, and economic freedom for all.

He often sails thousands of ocean miles while stopping in numerous foreign countries with only a few dollars in his pocket. As often as not, the pockets of his shorts rotted off months before. Why mend & repair what one doesn't have a need for? Dead Broke.

But—although Smith may have no money—he is not poor. He has his beloved boat—the limitless horizon as perpetual destination—and an ocean teeming with seafood. It is also almost impossible for John to walk into any sailor's bar from Nova Scotia to Brazil without having at least one person offering to buy him a drink.

But mostly what Captain John Smith is is irrepressible. He's simply impossible to dislike. He loves life so much—lives it so fully and has such a passion for each and every day—that just being enveloped in his aura of activity is fun. You can always get a 'contact high' from John. His mind is moving at a speed of a million nautical miles an hour... and it touches down like lightening strikes of illumination.

Of course, John has a few loose screws—clearly. Once, he contacted this reporter to journalistically 'cover' him as he discovered the Fountain of Youth which was guarded by a beautiful Brazilian Princess who possessed the Three Sacred Keys to the Three Sacred Gates...

...He's the sort of guy who will solemnly advise you to save your empty toothpaste tubes... and, of course, you carefully follow his sage advise... but he'll forget to tell you *why*, and you might be a tad too embarrassed to ask... (Author's Note to Himself: Remember to ask John *why* to save those stupid toothpaste tubes which are rapidly filling up my medicine cabinet...)

Just how John Smith came to be John Smith is harder to explain.

He's originally from Connecticut. That's not much help. In the 60's he was involved with the training of dolphins in Key West. It dawned on him that his students had it far more together than their teachers.

He arrived in the islands in the late 1960s. He soon purchased a 25 foot Seabird Yawl, and began exploring.

He's still at it. Sort of.

There were a couple of trimarans and a few odd monohulls between the Seabird Yawl and his purchasing *Mermaid of Carriacou*. The tri was struck by a freighter, and John nearly drowned. Instead, shipwrecked, he lived for awhile amid the tombstones in the Swedish Cemetery on St. Barths...

...The past is kind of fuzzy.

Parts of it are (gratefully) lost forever.

He headquartered out of St. Barths for awhile—back when that lovely island was a magic place filled with people of rare adventure. Everyone was so young, and free. Everyone would live forever. Tomorrow wouldn't/couldn't come. The wine and rum and champagne would never stop. Life was an endless, orgasmic party...

Of course, it did come to an end—reality reared its ugly head—but John had scented the freedom of the sea for too long to ever consider returning to normalcy.

Normal people seem to strike John as really/really/really weird. What motivates 'em? Why do they run so hard just to stay in place?

So John hung out with Jimmy Buffet, Foxy and Tess, Les Anderson, Bob Dylan, LouLou Magras, Neil Young, Mad Murphy, The Lov'n Spoonfuls, and other living legends who just happened to be Living the Life in Paradise.

He hauled vegetables, fished, and carried general cargo. A million and one money-making schemes were hatched—each was a Wild & Crazy adventure where (in the end) all concerned ended up with empty stomachs, pockets, and bank accounts.

Oh, well. It was fun—a Real Gas. It might have worked... but no matter, we've another idea for carrying palm trees northward, and exchanging them for...

On and on it went—and still goes.

John's entire life came to be somewhat of an art project. The *Mermaid of Carriacou* has no engine, no electronics, no nutt'n. There have been books written about her (see Douglas Pyle's "Clean Sweet Wind") and books written aboard her (see John Smith's own "Letters From Sinking Ships"). Pictures of her have appeared in National Geographic, numerous marine and travel mags, and the island of Grenada even issued a 35 cent stamp in her honor.

And the most amazing, glorious, astounding thing is that Smith &

the *Mermaid still* exist. He actually sails around saying things like "My Boat is Slow but The Sea Is Patient..." He appears to still believe that the pure force of Righteous Karma can carry you through. There aren't many John Smith's around anymore. Life in the electronic 90s have shut most of them down. But John Smith is still living The Dream. He has a wooden boat which usually doesn't leak faster than he can bail it out. The wind is free. A bag of brown rice is cheap. He doesn't have much else—but he's happy. And he has no plans to stop.

The View Through Rudy's Head

"The worst aspect of having John Steinbeck aboard for a couple of months," said his former Caribbean charter captain Rudy Thompson, "was provisioning the boat during the cruise. Nobody wanted to go ashore long enough to buy food because nobody wanted to miss a single one of his wonderful stories. We eventually asked John along while provisioning so we wouldn't all starve!"

Rudy Thompson—currently sixty-some years young—is a living legend in the Lesser Antilles. He arrived in the Virgin Islands in the late 1940's aboard a tiny Bahamian wooden sloop named *Jack Tarr* while looking for "...fun and adventure!" He found both while working on an inter-island freighter for "...five bucks a week, and all the sardines I could eat."

He soon entered the chartering game, and successfully skippered such revered early charter vessels as *Sea Saga, Tropic Bird,* and *Wind Song.* He chartered to a multitude of famous people, but clearly the highlight of his career was the four or five months with John Steinbeck in the mid 1950s between Trinidad and St. Thomas.

"Steinbeck had an incredible presence," recalled Rudy. "You could physically feel the force of his dynamic personality when he walked into a room. He was a big-boned, rough & tough *vital* man. Yet, he was always a gentlemen; always kind and considerate to others. His powers of observation were incredible."

"Within a couple of hours, he'd know more about a person than they'd ever revealed to another human being," said Rudy. "The best, most free-wheeling dinner conversations imaginable were orchestrated by John across our galley table."

"He drank a bottle of Cutty Sark a day. If there was any left in the bottle after he turned in, I was instructed to pour it overboard. Evidently he was cutting down. Yet I never saw him act tipsy or drunk. He had an enormous capacity for strong drink. He'd often steer for many hours at night—only a compass light and his bottle for company."

Rudy suffers from dyslexia, and thus was intimidated about corresponding with a Pulitzer Prize winner. "Steinbeck... like I said... was a true gentleman. To put me at my ease, he wrote me a long chatty letter which contained not a single word correctly spelled. I still have it; its one of my most cherished possessions."

Rudy Thompson recently raced his Tarten Ten 30 foot sloop *Cold Beer II* in the 1991 Antigua Sailing Week regatta. He finished well up in the racing fleet—just as he has for the last two decades he's participated in that highly competitive event. (He's also sailed in the

Olympics, the PanAm games, and five World Championships. When not racing fast, he slowly cruises. "I just love everything about sailing," he admits. "Nothing gives me more pleasure. I don't even find it tiring—only boredom or inactivity wearies me...") But whenever the Nor'east Trades rustle Rudy's hair, he thinks of John Steinbeck. "He often took notes. Everything was material for his work. Each morning before breakfast, he'd visit the 'throne'. While sitting there, he'd look out the small open porthole. He could see a circle of green island, the blue sea, another vessel, whatever. He always said that by seeking a smaller view, he could get a better picture of what he was seeing."

Rudy Thompson gazes out to sea, and says, softly, "He often joked he was going to write another book, and call it 'The View Through Rudy's Head.'"

John Steinbeck

Peter Holmberg & *Humbug 2*

J/29 Specifications

LOA	29' 6"	LWL 25' 0"	Beam 11' 1"
Draft	5' 8"	Ballast 2,100	Displacement 5,500
Sail area	471 sq feet		Design: Rodney Johnstone

The story of the J/29 *Humbug 2* is almost as interesting as the life story of her United States Virgin Island (USVI) 'bahn here' skipper Peter Holmberg. He purchased 'salvage rights' to the severely battered J/29 hull for $1,000 after she was declared a total loss in Hurricane Hugo. At the time (1989), he wasn't sure if he was buying her to strip or repair.

With the help of a few friends and a resin-splattered how-to book on fiberglass repair, Holmberg first made a temporary mold from the undamaged side. Then, he gently transferred that mold to the damaged area, and quickly patched the major five by ten foot hole in her port side. Inside the boat, he S-glassed back in her bilge stringers, and then firmly reattached her loose keel. Knowing that each ounce of extra weight would cost him dearly on the race course, Holmberg worked meticulously. "She came out about 20 to 25 pounds heavier than when she was factory new," Holmberg said. "Not too bad for amateurs."

Keeping the rest of the boat completely 'stock', he led his mainsheet, back stay adjuster, and traveler control to an area convenient to his helming position—and concentrated his other sail control lines at both his mast and his forward 'pit' areas to avoid too many people doing too many things in too small of an area.

For sails he turned to his good friend Dan Neri at Shore Sails in Newport. Working with an extremely limited budget—and using used & flawed fabric whenever possible—Neri built him a large-roached high performance 'spider cut' Mylar and Kevlar mainsail, a single all-purpose chute, and a Number #1 and Number #3 jib. "Most mains have to be cut 'user-friendly', but mine is not. It's a wonderful sail, but difficult to set. However, it allows me to sail competitively with only four sails, and yet be powered correctly in all conditions."

Holmberg's racing philosophy is simple—practice makes perfect. "My crew and I probably drill three times more than any other sailing team in the Caribbean. Everyone is always looking for some 'secret' edge, but it's really just old-fashioned hard work."

Holmberg is no stranger to the winner's circle. At nine years of age, he placed 13th out of 50 in the North America Sunfish Worlds. In college, he 'majored' in collegiate sailing. Returning to St. Thomas Yacht Club after graduation, he won nearly every race in the Caribbean—including its prestigious Rolex Cup.

In '84 at age 24 he represented the USVI at the Olympics in Finn Class, and came in 11th. Focusing his entire life on training for the Olympics, he won a Silver Medal (Finn) for the USVI in 1988 in Seoul, Korea.

Then he steered Bill Koch's Maxi *Matador 2* to victory in the 1989 Maxi World Championship, and stepped aboard Wictor Forss's *Carat VII* to win the 1990 International 50 World Cup. At some point, Peter Holmberg has—on a level playing field—beaten practically every top ranked 'driver' in the world.

"I think being a dinghy racer gave me an edge, even in the Maxis," said Holmberg recently. "Some of the other fellows hadn't been in a dinghy in ten years. They were thinking in terms of ten feet. I think in terms of inches. I'm a seat-of-the-pants, wind-on-my-face kind of sailor!"

His current goal is to be consistently rated among the top 20 match racers in the world. In 1991 he took a major step towards that goal by coming in second in the All Nations Cup in Bermuda. "I feel the future is in professionally-ranked small boat match racing. The Maxis and International 50s haven't really held media interest. Match racing is exciting, easy to understand, and capable of being captured on film. And the best part is that if you win—you make money instead of just spending it!"

Peter Holmberg at the helm of *Alinghi*

Bobby

He's known to everyone, prince and pauper alike, simply as 'Bobby' of "Bobby's Marine." He's man of immense reputation, vast experience, and considerable personal charm—and yet there is something about him which is difficult to define. There is nothing stereotypical about Bobby Velasquez. He is not an easy man to peg. He wears too many hats for that. It is as if he's a man from an early, simpler era in Sint Maarten history, when men were bigger, their problems smaller, and all things were possible. It doesn't seem possible that one man can combine so many diverse talents, bristle with such energy, or be at the hub of so many different organizational webs.

First and foremost, Bobby is a sailor. He was born in 1945, and practically grew up on the beach of Philipsburg. His family was poor but proud. His earliest recollections are of swimming, rowing, and working on his father's boats.

"I remember as a kid sailing with my father, Cap'n Austin Hodge. In the squalls or during the storms, he'd always personally take the wheel until his vessel was clear of danger. I'd sit in the doghouse, and watch his hands on the wheel. They were big, strong hands. I was never scared, really. He said there was danger at sea, but there were also ways of avoiding it. You had to be careful. My father would talk to me of the sea and sky, and how to read the stars. He'd teach me how to handle the ship and how to trim her sails. Even then, I loved everything about sailing.

"Sometimes, we'd bring home an apple from St. Kitts, a single juicy red apple. After dinner, we'd slice it up and divide it among the ten or twelve people in our family. The slice was thin, but the slice was good."

Bobby is also a highly successful businessman. His shipyard hauls about 500 boats a year. He currently has 68 employees. His marina has 55 slips. He dredges, he constructs, and he rebuilds large things daily. His tugs zip around the harbor as six of his cruise ship tenders glide by. In short: if it's marine-oriented and profitable, Bobby has a salt-stained finger in it.

"I started this operation with $400, with four hundred dollar bills. Each time I cashed one, my heart was in my throat. I had to do everything myself and make everything myself—for the simple reason that I could not afford to buy anything or hire anyone. It was difficult at first, but it got easier. Back then, of course, I was younger. I'd get up at dawn, and just couldn't wait to get at it. I've always wanted to build something today for tomorrow. I wanted to succeed, and was willing to work at it. I was offered various jobs in Holland— and could have worked elsewhere but I wanted to live here. I love Sint Maarten. I'm proud to be from Sint Maarten."

There's the three main elements of Bobby's larger-than-life personality—he loves Sint Maarten, he enjoys hard work, and he has always felt the obligation to earn the respect of honorable men like his father.

"My father went through hell for us, for our family. He risked his life, and worked hard for many years. He's a wonderful seaman and a fine sailor. He's 93 now. I've never wanted to do anything to disappoint him, to have anything reach his ears which would hurt him. That was, and still is, important to me."

The Philipsburg pier is named the Captain Austin Hodge Wharf after Bobby's father. This is appropriate—nobody used it more often to offload more cargo than Bobby's father.

Cap'n Hodge was a sailor all his life, too, just like his father before him. He captained one of the first Sint Maarten government boats, a small island sloop name *Trixy*. Then came the 72 foot schooner *Blue Peter*.

"The *Blue Peter* was built to yacht specifications in Nova Scotia," said Bobby. "She sailed with a crew of ten or twelve. She had an old Bhuda diesel engine that started on gas. She traveled up and down the islands for many years—and was very well known throughout the Lesser Antilles.

"Later, around 1952, my father quit the government. He built his own sailing cargo vessel right on the beach here in Philipsburg. He was a shipwright, too, same as his father. His boat's name was *Grace A Dieu* or Grace of God. She was the only boat to successfully ride out the hurricane of 1955 in Great Bay. My father put heavy weights on her anchor rodes, Spanish-style, and shifted her ballast forward so that she wouldn't have so much windage at the bow. It worked. That same storm took the *Blue Peter* ashore with her new captain...

"Back in those days, the sailing was really something. My father would regularly voyage to Santa Domingo, Curacao, Puerto Rico, and everywhere in between. We often sailed to St. Kitts together. We'd load 55 gallon drums of gas aboard. St. Kitts was the Miami of the Caribbean for many years. You could get Stanley tools and bicycles... you could get nearly anything on St. Kitts.

"They navigated by the wind and waves and sky back then. They had compasses, but not much else. They used the stars—the North star, the morning stars, and the Southern Cross. They knew when to tack depending on how close or far away a given star was to their forestay. They used a system of 'dead reckoning' to determine their position. To get from Santa Domingo to Sint Maarten, they'd sail something like, say, six hours to the southeast for every hour to the northeast. This would keep them pretty much on a direct track. They even accounted for the set of the current...

"They had to ride out a lot of hurricanes at sea because, of course, they had no weather warning systems back then. Once, my father and a 16 year old boy took *Blue Peter* through a hurricane, just the two of them. He lashed the boy to the foremast so he wouldn't get swept overboard... and left a machete tied close to his hand so he could cut himself free if they began to founder.

"They were some tough sailors back then. Even loading the boats wasn't easy. Sometimes cargo had to be lightered out on small boats, and transferred. The Philipsburg Town Wharf which now bears my father's name had an old manual hand crane on it, that was it. Sailing was hard work, whether you were at sea or in port. Sometimes the boats leaked in the storms, and the crews had to man those old deck-style pitcher pumps with eight foot long handles..."

For young Bobby, going to sea was a way of proving he was a man. Even as a young boy he jumped at any chance to work on the boats. He'd row out to his father's craft each day to wet the decks down so they wouldn't dry out in the hot sun. He'd make sure she always had a kerosene anchor light hoisted in her rigging at dusk. He had a little sailing dinghy, and would haul fish traps in his spare time. Every Saturday, he'd sail over to the Oyster Pond area with fresh water for his family's cattle. He particularly enjoyed sailing on the windward side of Sint Maarten. It was exciting when the wind was up.

"I enjoyed the responsibility. I loved everything about it. I couldn't seem to learn enough. I'd sail with my father to St. Kitts, and he'd teach me to the best of his ability. I learned knots, and how to splice rope and wire from him. When I grew older, he taught me a deep respect for tools. He taught me how to swing an adze and use a hand saw, and if he ever found me goofing around with a tool or using it in an improper manner—boy, I'd get my hands slapped fast!"

At 16, after attending school locally at the St. Joseph Convent, Bobby went to college in Curacao for six years. He studied engineering, but boats were never far from his mind. He also studied in Miami for two years. He enjoyed his studies and all his travels (as one would expect of a young man who held both a French and a Dutch passport and spoke four languages) but eventually he longed to return home. "I missed Sint Maarten. This is where I belong, where my family is, where I love."

As soon as he got back on the island, he got back into boats. He chartered the 41 foot trimaran named *Great Eagle* in 1967, and the following year skippered a Columbia 36 named *Praywind*. In between chartering, he obtained his U.S. Coast Guard Captain's License, and did a number of deliveries from Puerto Rico and the States. It was during this time that his interest in sportfishing blossomed, and he soon developed quite a reputation among the sportfishermen of Puerto Rico, many of whom remain both friends and customers to this day.

He started Bobby's Marine back in 1971. It started out as Bobby's Yacht Service. He leased the land, and built a small building on it. Next, he worked on the breakwater. He personally man-handled many of the heavy rocks into place. It was hot, tiring, difficult work.

Finally, in 1974, he began work on the massive railway. "We had to improvise because we didn't have any of the proper heavy equipment back then. I built the main supports for the tracks of the railway out of reinforced concrete, and then pushed them into the water with a front-loader. We only broke one, and that one we quickly patched. We'd constantly run into construction problems, but we'd just figure out a way around them, we'd just keep at it until it was done."

After the shipyard was up and running, Bobby turned his attention to the marina. "At that point there was a barge, crane, and pile-driver from Holland here in Sint Maarten to work on the cruise ship pier. I desperately needed a large pile-driver to build my docks. So I offered them a deal. I'd allow them to use my yard as a staging area if they'd allow me to use their heavy equipment for a single 24 hour period."

It was a classic Bobby-the-Builder story, another instant engineering marvel. "We worked like dogs to get everything ready. Remember, we only had 24 hours to set all those pilings. All of our materials were preset, pre-measured, pre-cut, pre-marked, and pre-stacked. The crane showed up and we all worked around the clock—both in and out of the water. By the following day, we had all the piles, almost 30 of them, driven for the dock. It took a lot of time to eventually finish the project, but the most important, most difficult part took place on a single day—using equipment I could never have afforded to hire..."

The railway hauled boats till 1982. It repaid its modest investment many times over. Then Bobby purchased a 50 ton Travel Lift—another first in the Caribbean. Today, the yard features a 90 ton Travel Lift, easily the largest in the Caribbean. It can handle a boat up to 22 feet wide. For the growing number of Sint Maarten multihulls which are beamier than 22 feet, Bobby has a large crane to effortlessly pluck them ashore.

"I've always aimed for a full service operation," said Bobby. "We can do just about anything here—engine rebuilds, welding, custom metal work, shipwright service, osmosis work, electrical repair, fiberglass work, sail repair, electronic service... We've got a good restaurant, a convenience store... even a laundry!"

Although his staff of 68 is primarily made up of locals, he's got workers from around the world. "I'm very fussy about the quality of work we do. You can't succeed in this business without repeat customers. You have to do good work at reasonable prices. I've got a good operation here, a good team, and I want it to stay that way. I've got repeat customers that come from down-island and from Puerto Rico year after year... because they know they'll be treated well. I'm always available, always ready to help my customers. If something isn't right, we make it right. I want my customers to leave happy and come back next time."

Bobby's customers are as diverse as his employees. A frugal sea-gypsy might find his modest boat propped up between an expensive 65 foot gold-plated ocean racer from Monaco and a broken down local fishing boat from Carriacou. Everyone gets treated the same at Bobby's, everyone enjoys the same level of service.

Another example of Bobby's wide-ranging interests and abilities: he recently won a major fishing tournament in Antigua aboard his Stryker Sportfisher *Bonhomme Richard* and shortly thereafter placed second in class during the Heineken Regatta about his Heineken-sponsored Kelt 10M sloop named *My Way*.

"I enjoy sailboat racing," said Bobby. "We have a lot of fun. We do the local Wednesday night races, and some of the more serious regattas. I've got a good crew, and we win our fair share."

Of course, Bobby has many other interests besides sailing. He's a community activist who feels that since Sint Maarten has given him so much, he's obligated to pay back the community in a number of different ways.

He's currently president of the Sint Maarten Red Cross, a group he was instrumental in founding 18 years ago. He also sits on the board of the Philipsburg Management Association, a volunteer citizen's organization which works closely with both the government and the private sector for, Bobby hopes, the good of all.

"I'm confident of Sint Maarten's future. We're a unique island, and we have much to offer. Our 'free port' status is the main reason we've been able to come so far so fast. Right now, well, we've got some problems and a lot of little things aren't quite right, but I'm sure that we'll get the island back on course soon. Things will work out."

While Bobby's wide field of vision encompasses just about everything concerning Sint Maarten, his focus always returns to the sea. Twelve years ago he founded the Sint Maarten Sea Rescue Foundation. It currently has two fully equipped rescue boats, and has saved many lives. "It's an all volunteer group," according to Bobby. "We can usually have a boat underway within five minutes of an emergency call.

We wear beepers, and there's about fifteen of us, four of which have some medical training."

Bobby donates the dock space, maintenance costs, and fuel for the boats. "Lots of people and organizations help out Sea Rescue. The local support has been wonderful. Over the years the Food Center has been particularly generous. We have a charity fishing tournament each June, and that's a major source of funding. We manage to get by."

Bobby admits that as he gets older it gets tougher to juggle so many different tasks. Still, he harbors some ambitious plans. "I want to extend my breakwater and eventually pave the entire yard. We're going to be expanding our fleet of cruise ship tenders from six to eight—we can't seem to buy them fast enough. And if I get any free time away from the office, I'd love to take an extended cruise of the West Coast of the United States..."

That's typical Bobby. He's always working on a number of major projects at the same time, always building for the future, always dreaming the next dream.

Could a youngster today follow in his foot steps? Could Bobby accomplish today what he did yesterday?

"Absolutely," said Bobby. "The marine industry here in Sint Maarten offers a number of business opportunities—golden opportunities—for a young fellow who wants to work hard. But you have to be ambitious, you have to give it your all. You can't wait for someone to hand it to you, because no one ever will."

SERIOUS T'INGS

Cap'n Fatty in the Virgin Islands

Nirvana Bay

Once upon a time—long long ago in the 1980's—there was a lonely harbor in the Virgin Islands called Nirvana Bay. There was no decent road leading to it, it was surrounded by swamp, and the beach was honest mud. If the tradewinds faltered, it got rolly in the anchorage. Only a few open fishing boats lined its shore.

Then the surrounding harbors started to bulge, and a few cruising vessels began to anchor in Nirvana Bay. They were sailors from all over the world, friendly, honest & open and they soon formed a little live-aboard community. The bay was quiet, and a fine place to stare up at God's stars and listen to His crickets chirp.

They shared their food, love, and laughter. Their kids mingled. They watched out for each other in many large (and small) ways. Their parties, hospitality, and comradery became deservedly well-known. They were very proud of their watery little brotherhood, and enjoyed sharing it.

Then one morning, after a wonderful party aboard a French boat named *Life's A Beach*, they all awoke to a collective horrible hang-over. Bang/bang/BANG! They stuck their heads out of their hatches and stared dully at the shore where a bright yellow pile-driver was ruining their day.

Sure, they went to all the local community meetings—along with the Nirvana Home Owners Association—and listened to the resort developer's spiel. "The resort will be good for everyone. The boaters will be able to use the hotel dock to tie up their dinghies, the pool can be used to teach West Indian youngsters to swim—and we will put in sidewalks along the main road ..."

The boaters were taxpayers, citizens, and voters like everyone else, and they weren't against jobs, progress, or developers. They didn't protest. Many actually got well-paying jobs building the resort.

Hundreds of hotel units, meeting rooms, and condos sprang up from the swamp. Barge after barge after barge of pristine Barbados sand was dumped upon the muddy shore. Palms trees waved. It was Paradise, alright—and only 500 bucks a night.

The hotel opened amid much fanfare and the harbor suddenly got real crowded. Charter boats, dive boats, ferries, water taxis, and rental boats all crowded in.

All these power vessels had propellers and their 'prop wash' stirred up the bottom so much that the water soon became cloudy. Grain by grain, all that imported Barbados beach sand started shoaling the bay. The resort's sewage treatment plant didn't work correctly immediately. So around 2 a.m. each evening there was a certain stench... and the resort owners held their noses and pointed to the boats.

Hotel guests on windsurfers, Sunfish, rowboats, jetskis, and outboards shot through the teeming harbor like a wacky nautical pinball game, bouncing off the boats for extra points.

The hotel's landscaping was like Eden, but that takes a lot of chemicals and fertilizer to maintain. Soon the beach was covered with smelly green slime. Bulldozers were forced to push the stinking mess aside each morning. The resort's bright illumination blanked out the stars at night, and the dance bands & tourist music drowned out the soft sounds of the crickets chirping.

Many boaters thought the resort was A Great Evil. They demanded the resort keep its promises. But the resort put an "X" through its sign out front, changed its named, and kept staring at its short-term bottom line. (It did some good deeds, too— but how easy to forget...)

Many of the boaters were just as evil as the resort. Some didn't pay their fair share —refused to get mooring permits or register their vessels locally. Some sailors *did* purchase moorings, and then rented them out for personal profit. One charter company illegally wrangled control of a dozen of them, and leased them out to rich New Yorkers for mega-bucks. Everybody has a bottom line to watch.

Many of the new arrivals in the bay weren't cruising sailors or yachtsman—but landsman who used their vessels merely as floating abodes. Some of the vessels were total wrecks, without engine, mast, nor oar.

One fellow 'collected' boats without titles. Another was suspected of "...teef'n." One guy got drunk, tossed his lady overboard, and took potshots at her as she swam away. Our society isn't perfect; neither are boaters.

The cold war between boaters and the resort began to heat up. The hotel attempted to drive the dinghies off the beach. (Gasp!) The more radical elements of the marine community jumped to the fore front of the fray and convinced the resort that the boaters were (indeed!) freeloaders, bums, and jerks.

Lines and circles in the beach sand were drawn. Cliques clicked. Groups formed. Fingers pointed. Lies were told. Truth varnished. Everyone shouted; no one listened.

And so it came to pass a few weeks ago that a blond-bearded sailor—one of the original live-aboards who had helped built the resort—catted up his anchor rode for the very last time. His wife, with a fat baby suckling at her plump breast, was at the schooner's wheel. They were moving to Nevis, a quiet little island just over the horizon. A new resort was going up, and there was plenty of honest work available.

As they steamed out of the harbor, an arriving vessel hailed them. "Is this Nirvana Bay?" it asked.

"Not any more," was the reply.

The Romance and the Reality
of being a Caribbean Charter Captain

We've all had The Idea.

Chuck it. Chop our docklines. Toss aside the power cord. Flee to the Caribbean. Become a Sea Gypsy. Cruise only where wind, weather, and whim dictate. March to our own salt-stained drummer. And—when the cruising kitty is depleted of Freedom Chips—pick up a few charters. Literally become paid to play.

"Aye, Matey! Won't it be grand!"

The possibility is especially alluring to knowledgeable sailors who have vacationed aboard a fully-crewed charter boat in the Caribbean. They've already tasted sailing at its pampered best—seen the palm-fronded beaches waving welcome —watched the sun hiss into the tropical sea astern. They've experienced that priceless sense of peace only an anchored vessel in Paradise can provide. They know The Dream can be real.

They also remember how contented their skipper appeared to be as he lounged around the cockpit. How naturally he seemed to move with the vessel—and how the boat naturally seemed to move with him. And they've thought, "Why not me? If this man can lead such a story-book existence—why not me?"

"I too came to the Caribbean chasing a dream," admitted Captain Ben Sheets recently as he sat in the shade of a palm tree in the courtyard of Yacht Haven Marina on St. Thomas. "My dream was to sail around the world while chartering. I rapidly discovered—at least for me, at that time, in that vessel—the idea wasn't practical."

Sheets, outgoing president of the Virgin Islands Charteryacht League (VICL)—a non-profit association of 160 professional captains soon adjusted his private dream to the realities of the marketplace. After three years of chartering his 85 foot wooden yawl *Royono* in the Virgins, he became captain of *Margin Call*, a 74 foot Ted Hood designed Little Harbor.

Along with wife Sarah, who is a graduate of the Culinary Institute of America, a licensed USCG captain in her own right, and also Vice-President of the Professional Yacht Chef's Association; Captain Sheets now heads up one of the most respected chartering teams in the business. He loves his job, and is not shy admitting it. Yet when asked to briefly sum up his job, he chose the two words almost universally echoed by his fellow captains. "Hard work!"

If a professional charter captain is doing his job perfectly, his guests are rarely aware he's doing it at all. Moving the boat—sailing, seamanship, and safety— are just small elements within the larger picture. Ferry captains provide transportation. Charter yacht skippers provide unforgettable sailing vacations at an affordable price to a wide variety of people—experiences so unique and captivating that guests evolve into friends who will return year after year to 'visit'.

The task is not an easy one. It requires a true "Jack-Tarr-of-All-Trades"—a special mix of sailor, host, entertainer, business man, diplomat, travel guide, plumber, electrician, diesel mechanic, sea-faring psychologist, and friend. The skipper must inspire confidence, allay fears, and be sensitive to the mood, talents, and interests of his guests. He should have a sense of theatre. The one mandatory attribute a charter captain must have, besides passing the USCG's captain's test and having 360 documented days of sea time, is a genuine, unforced, non-critical love for his fellow man.

Take Dyke and Inga Wilmerding, for instance. They've been doing term charters in the Virgins for over 23 years now, first on their classic Alden schooner *Mandoo*, and now on their Gallant 57 *Zulu Warrior*. Many of their current guests first stepped aboard years ago. This summer, a doctor from Detroit is giving them the ultimate compliment—rebooking for the 8th time.

Dyke and Inga hesitated when asked for the two biggest reasons for their success. Finally, Dyke mumbled something vague about how well *Zulu Warrior* sails, and how lovely the islands are. When asked the same question, one of their many satisfied guests immediately responded, "Dyke and Inga!"

One long time professional charterboat captain said that he was "running the world's smallest, most exclusive hotel with the tiniest staff and budget imaginable, while providing the most personalized service conceivable."

The business side of chartering is sobering, especially in a country where both the ice and a Coke costs more than the rum.

Very few charter boats turn a reasonable profit for money invested. If past trends hold true, less than half the skippers currently chartering today will be active in four years. Most well-found, well maintained charter vessels must charter 10-12 weeks— that's nearly 3 solid months of back-to-back 24 hour workdays—just to break even.

The costs of owning and operating a charter boat is high. A bag of groceries costs 38% more in St. Thomas than it does in Washington, D.C. Fresh water on nearby St. John, if available, goes for $.15 a gallon, or $60.00 for 400 gallons. On the island of Bequia, a standard one inch shaft zinc was recently spotted for sale at $28.50. An effective, full color advertising brochure costs between $5,000 and $9,000. Like any business, there are local licenses, taxes, and fees which must be paid. Don't forget brokerage, haul-out, sail, diesel, and general maintenance costs—all must be factored into the picture. What about the cost of laundry, linens, and crew uniforms? Most boats spend between $800 to $1,200 to provision for a week for six people. Some boats spend double that. What's the bottom line? "I always seem to spend just a little bit more than I take in," confessed one skipper with a sigh.

The annual insurance bill on Captain Ben Sheet's 74 foot *Margin Call* is $20,000. A few months ago, he spent $26,000 dollars on repairs, replacements, maintenance, and capital improvements within a single 30 day period. True, *Margin Call* charters for over $10,000 a week, and rarely sits idle for long—but still the numbers are astounding.

Then there is the growing list of sea-going 'toys' being offered by many of the newer vessels. Ski boats, wind surfers, scuba gear, underwater scooters, motorized surfboards, video cameras, VCRs, jet-skis, and cellular phones all cost money to purchase, maintain, and replace.

Comparing operating costs, chartering fees, and profit among vessels is difficult. Each vessel is its own little company, as individualistic as its skipper.

For the sake of comparison, let's take a look at a 'typical' 46 foot sloop worth $160,000 which charters to four people for $3,746 a week.

(Again: operating costs vary. The average charter boat charges $5,700 a week, or between $850 and $1,500 per person per week, according to David Crook, current president of the VICL. Similar sized vessels operating in the same waters can and do spend widely different amounts in each category.)

Before the vessel even leaves the dock, it has to pay approximately $3,200 for insurance, $4,600 for annual maintenance, $1,174 in promotion and advertising fees, $1,815 in office and administration costs, and $14,400 in capital costs. (In this example, capital costs are equal to the amount $160,000
would earn at 9% interest.) All this adds up to $25,189 of fixed annual operating 'expenses'.

By the end of the first charter, the vessel has had to lay out another $53 for dockage, $562 for a broker, $50 for fuel, and $853 for provisions and incidentals. That's another $1,518—for a total operating cost of $26,707. Subtract the $3,747 charter fee, and the business is in the red for $22,960.

Assuming maintenance, promotion, and office expenses add on another $50 to $100 each week, the break-even point comes during the 12th week of chartering— when a profit of $938 is realized. By the 21st week, the profit is $20,385.

The wear and tear on the vessel is obvious. It can be measured in dollars and cents. The stress on the crew is more difficult to quantify, yet can be equally severe.

There's little privacy. Captain and cooks soon learn how to have 30 second silent arguments. Although 95% of the people who charter are delightful, there is the occasional drunk, the soon-to-be-divorced couple, the people who can't sleep without the hum of a city in their ears. "Each season I have one 'stare
at your toes and bite your tongue' charter," confesses one skipper.

Chartering a vessel 20 weeks in a year is difficult. Much of the work needs to be done while off-charter. You can't revarnish the galley table during dinner. Like any small business, there's paperwork involved: record keeping, customs and immigration, follow-up letters and pictures to previous guests, food preference sheets, correspondence, menu planning, maintenance schedules, etc.   Yet despite all these negatives, there are plenty of great charter captains around. Why?

"Freedom," said VICL Captain Mike White of *Esprit*, a Jeanneau 45. "It's a tough business, but a great life style."

Most professional captains agree. Few speak of money; many admit their tips are an important addition to their income. Depending on an individual's financial situation, running a charter business can have certain tax advantages. It is difficult to spend money while on charter, so considerable savings can result from a relatively modest income. Many owners have much larger, more expensive vessels than they could afford if they were in another line of business making an equal amount of money.

But the real benefit of chartering is the experience itself. "I get to continuously see the islands anew through the eyes of my guests," says VICL Captain George Brown of the Morgan Out Islands 41 *Thorobred*.

"I'm having a ball," says Captain Steve Macek of the Camper Nicholson 60 *Patricia Gayle III*. "My guests are no different from my friends. I don't have to commute too far to get to work. I get to sail, swim, travel, party—and I even get a pay check! Life couldn't get much better."

The chartering business has come a long way since Captain Basil Symonette of *Sea Saga* first got paid to sail a couple of tourists around St. John back in the '40s, or since Captain Dick Avery charged $6.00 per person per day for food aboard his schooner *Victoria* back in the '50's, or since Captain Rudy Thompson listened to John Steinbeck spinning sea-yarns back in the '60s. A lot of water has passed under the keel since men like Neil Lewis of *Chiquita*, Bill Beer of *True Love*, Don Street of *Iolaire*, and Dyke Wilmerding of *Mandoo* pioneered the infant industry so many years ago.

But the more things change; the more they stay the same. The reasons people chartered in the '50s are identical to the reasons people charter in the '80s. The wind and the sea and the sky haven't changed. The ocean still calls. Salt air heals. Seagulls laugh.

For a few special sailors, the life of a charter captain in Paradise *is* Paradise. Once at sea, their worldly cares, along with their guest's, disappear astern. Their two biggest joys in life, sailing and people, combine daily in an endless parade of palm-framed memories. In the final analysis, they are as romantic as their guests. They delight in being 'paid to play,' no matter how much hard work it entails.

And miracles still happen. Captain Ben Sheets, the man who set out to circumnavigate under charter, will soon achieve more than half of his goal. He is currently in the Far East, overseeing the construction of a new 100-plus foot sailing vessel. Upon completion, he'll leisurely deliver her back to the Caribbean, occasionally chartering along the way.

Tough job, but somebody's got to do it.

Morgan Goodlander and his wife Beatrice
enjoy a charter in the Virgin Islands.

Carmen

Carmen was a quiet, well-behaved child. Perhaps almost too well-behaved. She seem far older and mature than her seven years warranted. She seemed to carry within her a certain sad wisdom. Perhaps the death of her mother while Carmen was still nursing had a dampening effect on her dark-eyed personality. Who can say?

I liked her enough to often invite her to tag along with me as I went into town. I've never done this before with any child who was not flesh of my blood. Carmen seemed grateful. Her eyes would light up as I swung my dinghy alongside her father's boat. "Can Carmen come with me into town? We'll stop for an ice cream cone, and then meet my daughter's school bus. They can play together..."

"Please, papa," she'd implore him. He always allowed her these brief freedoms.

I liked Carmen so much I tentatively discussed informally 'adopting' her with my wife. She was as pretty as a China doll. She could attend Pine Peace School, and live with us. Perhaps it was just idle chatter on my part.

Carmen lived aboard an engineless 49 foot wooden sailing vessel named *L'Artemis*. It was the same boat her mother had fallen overboard from, and drowned. Carmen's mother (Chinese) was her father's second wife. His first had also gotten knocked overboard and drowned at sea.

Carmen's father, a man call Tangvald from Norway, was a man of the sea. He and I had much in common. We'd both built boats, sailed oceans, and raised our daughters aboard. We didn't have inboard engines on our vessels. We were both marine magazine writers and book authors. We hit it off pretty good; had some nice cockpit dinners together.

But Tangvald shunned the shore. He liked to stay aboard his vessel. He only went into town if absolutely necessary. The noise, traffic, and confusion appeared to scare him. His eyes would blink, and his nose would flare.

He seemed more a solitary mountain man than an international yachtsman who lived aboard a boat while single-handedly raising his daughter.

Carmen didn't talk much about the boat. She just wanted to be a child. Play with other kids. Learn the names of the Ninja Turtles. Eat candy. Have fun. Laugh.

One evening my wife Carolyn and I were sitting together in our cockpit. *L'Artemis* was anchored astern of us. We could see the soft glow of its kerosene lamps. I blurted out, "I like Tangvald, but he's a selfish man, isn't he?"

My wife didn't respond for a long time. Finally, "Yes."

We talked about it then; about Carmen. Her father loved her deeply; and she loved him. They worried about each other. America was filled with unwanted and unloved children. Wasn't Carmen better off than they? So what if her clothes were shabby; she was clean. Who were we to judge their lives through the shaded prism of *our* parent's values?

Larry and Leonora Best of the ketch *Perseverance* helped Tangvald sail his boat out of Great Cruz Bay, heading westward for Culebra. (Tangvald's fifteen year old son Thomas apparently lived there.) Carmen was belowdecks when both Larry and Leonora hopped back into their small dinghy and said good bye. "It was an eerie feeling," Leonora told me later that same day. "I didn't want to leave her. I felt terrible."

They made it safely to Culebra. A few months later I saw a small classified newspaper advertisement. Tangvald was looking for another wife, another mother for Carmen. I shivered.

Two or three weeks ago—give or take—Tangvald, his son Thomas, and Carmen left Puerto Rico for the summer. They sailed southward. I assume they were attempting to hole-up in Venezuela for hurricane season.

Three or four days out, they got into heavy weather along the north coast of Bonaire. Reports are sketchy. I do not know what happened, but the drowned bodies of Carmen and Tangvald washed ashore on the rocks of Punta Blancu. (Thomas was reported to have survived, and is currently hospitalized.)

I once saw a painting by an artist named Ivan Albright. It was a weathered hand reaching out to a tattered funeral wreath upon a closed door. It's title was, "That Which I Should Have Done, I Did Not Do."

But modern life is a complex affair. Its answers often elude us. The past is over. Unchangeable. But I sincerely wish I could have hugged Carmen more often, bought her more ice cream, and lovingly watched her blossom into womanhood.

On Squalls, Agony, and Ego

Over the course of the last 15 years of being a professional marine journalist, there are few aspects of sailing which I have not written about extensively. The two subjects to which I've probably devoted the most printer's ink are safety and seamanship.

Recently I wrote a story with these lines: "Most boats are lost because of their crew's impatience. The skipper, in his haste to get ashore, puts his vessel in too much danger as he approaches the coast. Instead of remaining offshore in relative safety, he opts to shoot the risky harbor entrance in less than ideal conditions. Most of the time, of course, he pulls it off. But occasionally, tragically, he does not. For an offshore sailor, haste often makes waste."

Another factor which I've rallied against is macho-ness and ego. "The fool believes that he can put his boat in danger, and get away with it. The seasoned sailor attempts to never put his vessel in any significant danger, while continuously thinking of what he would do if it suddenly was."

Despite all of the above — and perhaps because it is easier to preach than to learn — I recently found myself violating both principals.

I was single-handing my 38 foot engineless sloop from St. John to Jost Van Dyke to attend the 20th annual Foxy's Wooden Boat Regatta. The journey was only about 15 miles. It usually takes me about three hours. With a little luck, I might do it on a single starboard tack. It was daylight, and I was in familiar waters. I'd just sailed my vessel almost 1,000 miles within the month. To put it mildly, I was confident.

I sailed off my mooring without mishap, and was soon squared away. There was very little wind, and I was occasionally becalmed. There was a strong current against me, but I was able to make some headway against it despite my boat's bottom being somewhat foul. I figured the current would add an hour or two on the trip. Big deal.

At one point, I had to pass between the island of Lovango and Rata Cay. This is called Windward Passage, and of course, my course was dead to windward. Unfortunately, the narrowing of the passage made the current speed up considerably, and I could barely make any headway against it. Each tack would only gain me 20 or 30 feet. It was wearying, mentally and physically. I tacked and tacked and tacked. An hour went by. I was almost through the cut, then I *was* through... and almost clear away... and the wind dropped and the current strengthened and I was swept back backwards through the cut practically to where I started.

Of course, there were boats all around me, but they had engines. Once they'd hit the increased current, they'd crank up for a few minutes and nonchalantly power beyond it to the smooth water ahead. It was demoralizing to watch them, one after the other, wiggle through and proceed while I was, despite my ceaseless tacking/tacking/tacking, still going nowhere fast.

All I could do was to keep trying, and that is what I did. The winds were light, but there were thunder squalls all around me. I prayed for some wind.

Amazingly, I got it. I started sailing fast, tacking easily against the current, just skirting the breaking rocks on each side of the passage, nearly free at last!

Then suddenly I saw the squall ahead. It was big and black and scary-looking. I hoped I would be through the passage before it was upon me, but no such luck.

Suddenly I was in almost 30 knots of wind (and a blinding rain) with my full mainsail up! A higher gust hit me then, my vessel lurched its loo-ard rail into the water, and then another gust rocked us... and I had no choice, I had to tuck a couple of reefs (reduce) into my mainsail or I'd lose the mast... and so with a heavy heart I turned back downwind, raced at great speed to where I'd started from the first and second times, and grimly double-reefed my mainsail.

And started again. This time I was determined to make it, come hell or high water.

I had about twenty knots of wind, plenty to push me against the current, even with the current-exaggerated steep waves. Half an hour later I was almost through the cut, with only another ten minutes or so to go, when I got nailed by a truly ferocious squall.

It couldn't have happened at a worst time. I was only a couple of hundred yards off the rock-bound shore of the island of Lovango. Despite my double-reefed mainsail, I was heeled far, far too much, so I partially rolled up my roller furling headsail. For a few horrifying moments, the lashing rain reduced my visibility from endless to nearly zero. I knew that the crashing rocks of Lavango were within stone throwing distance on my portside, but I could not see them.

I was directly to windward of the island, and it was too close to loo-ward—and the wind and the currently were slowly and unstoppably pushing me sideways into it. It was a horrible feeling. My stomach was in knots, and I was gasping for air. I would have to tack soon, or I'd lose the boat. I prayed for the 35 knot wind to drop, but it did not. If anything, it increased in strength. The tops of the waves were blowing off. My rigging was screaming and moaning. I was beginning to be truly scared, to think I might not make it. I had to tack, had to. There was no room to gybe. I had to tack, and if she wouldn't tack she'd be lost.

I tried to tack, and failed. I couldn't believe it. Oh, God! It was unbelievable. The rocks were only 125 yards away! I tried to tack again, and failed! We were going to strike! I had to tack, HAD TO TACK... so I bore away towards the rocks to pick up as much speed as possible, threw the helm over, and attempted to make my boat's bow tack through sheer force of will... but it would not do so.

We were within a hundred feet of the rocks now. There was no hope. She would strike, be holed, and sink. DAMN!

I ran forward without rational thought, casting off the jib and main sheets as I went passed. I dragged my knife across the main halyard to cut down the mainsail, cut the tie-down to my anchor to release it into the sea, and (sobbing or gasping for breath, I'm not sure which) grabbed the tag-line of the genoa and furled it frantically.

My anchor line was hissing out of the hawse hole like a hot snake. There were coral heads around me. I was in shallow water. The wind was still 30 knots, gusting, and the seas were building. This would never work. I was dreaming. This was stupid. I'd lost my boat, my home, every single thing my wife and I owned...

There were the rocks, just astern of me. They were breaking. They were huge. They looked so evil, so heartless, so mean. When the transom of my boat was within 25 feet of them, 'twanginnnggg!' went my anchor line, and my jaw dropped in amazement as I realized we were holding.

It seemed impossible. I shoved another anchor over, before I realized that it would never have a chance to take up its slack before the boat would be holed if my current anchor dragged even a few feet.

The situation was totally untenable. I couldn't possibly stay here for long. I only had down a light lunch hook, for gosh sakes. Maybe it was chafing on coral right now, right this second. Maybe it would snap any moment...

Frantically, I squared away the boat, made it shipshape again. I had to sail away, but how? Since I'd cut my main halyard, I only had the use of my headsail. I couldn't go to windward in high winds with only a jib... I was screwed, doomed, a rat-in-a-trap...

Suddenly, there was a lull in the wind. It went from 35 knots to a mere 18 knots. I looked to windward, and there was another squall fast approaching which looked just as bad as the last or perhaps even worse. I'd have to make my move now, right now! There was no time to think, to carefully consider... I only had a few minutes before it hit...

I grabbed a cockpit line, lashed it on a strong cleat, and ran it outside of everything up to my anchor line on the bow. The squall was almost upon me. With a whimper of near panic, I cast off the anchor line from the bow. I ran aft as my boat lurked backwards, the anchor line on her port quarter became taut, and her bow began to pay off to starboard. I waited maybe two, three seconds, released the headsail tag line, popped out the jib, and cut the cockpit anchor line with a single swipe of my well-used knife. Suddenly I was free! I was sailing, sailing paralleling the coast, working slightly away from the rocks... making it, making it, making it, I'M GONNA MAKE IT..!

And then I was back through the passage again, and there was no immediate lee shore, absolutely no danger, and another 35 knot squall lashed at me and I was laughing and ranting and crying... and chanting over and over, "God, that was close! Too close! Boy-oh-boy, that was close! Gee-zuss! WOW!!!! Close/close/CLOSE!" as my knees knocked and head ached and every muscles in my body decided that, now, finally, it was okay to cramp-up... and I was oh-so-happy-to-be-alive-with-my-vessel-under-me.

The point of the above story is not to yet again use the pages of this fine publication to inform you of what a stone-cold idiot I am—but to honestly convey what can happen when you violate some basic rules of seamanship.

I should have never been single-handing an engineless boat in a narrow cut with an adverse current on a dead lee shore while surrounded by severe squalls. Never.

All I had to do was wait a couple of hours, and the squalls would have disappeared and the current would have been *with* me instead of against me and the rain would have been long gone...

...but instead, because I'd been pushed back twice already, I, Mister Macho, decided to go for it 'come hell or high water!'

And I nearly lost my boat (and, perhaps, my life) because of such a foolish, immature decision.

They say we 'live and learn' but I'm not sure that's true. My personal history seems to confirm just the opposite. I never seem to grow bored of endlessly repeating the same mistakes.

But this recent lesson was driven home in the most gut-wrenching, bowel-loosening manner possible without a major tragedy resulting — and thus I promise publicly to never, ever take such a foolish risk again. And *this* time I mean it!

Captain Larry Got Stoned

Traditionally, newspaper journalists like to begin their first column of a New Year on a decidedly upbeat note. Something with a sappy, hopeful, and idealistic headline, like "Don't worry; be happy—the best is yet to come!"

But I am unable to do this because my best friend, Captain Larry Best of the yacht *Perseverance*, got stoned.

I don't mean he got high on drugs, I mean he was assaulted without provocation with rocks. By a large (7-10) group of brazen teenagers. On a heavily traveled public road. At seven o'clock in the evening. While trudging home from a hard day at work. On the once tranquil island of St. John.

"Sticks and stones will break my bones, but names will never hurt me" is still true. When the group of youngsters started following him, Larry wasn't scared. After all, this was St. John, USVI. Paradise. When they started saying nasty things to scare and intimidate him—he was understandably concerned, but still not too panicky. One of the group then asked him, "You scared, mon?" and Larry said, his voice, beginning to shake with fear, "Naw, you guys are all right."

But they weren't 'all right'. They were evil. First a small little pebble—so tiny it could barely hurt a flea—sailed harmlessly passed Larry's head. Then another missed. Then a larger one. He turned to protect his face; started walking briskly away. More stones; bigger stones now flew. Larry started running. The gang of kids gave chase. They started howling. Their stones were raining harmlessly around him... and then one large, hard-driven rock cut deeply into his fleeing back—and Larry was suddenly running/running/running for his very life.

Let me tell you a little about Lawrence T. Best. It's kind of ironic. Larry is an honest-to-goodness pacifist. Raised a Quaker, he served his country as a conscientious objector during the Vietnam war. He's from a peaceful little New England town, son of a highly liberal book editor, and works locally as a professional land surveyor. Larry and his family have marched against war, against racism, against violence many times.

A number of years ago, Larry built a boat with his own two hands. He had a dream. He wanted to sail to Paradise. It took him almost ten years of continuous back-breaking toil to build his boat. During that time, he kept getting letters from this reporter—factually reporting on how wonderful the island of St. John was, how remarkably kind were her many-hued, loving residents, how very high the quality of life on this blessed rock truly was. "Come on down, Larry! You'll love it."

And so it all came to pass. Larry rented out his nice New England home, moved his wife Leonora aboard their stout boat, and sailed down to Paradise. He obeyed all the rules, happily paid his societal dues in every conceivable way, and loved it.

Up until that first tiny pebble sailed harmlessly passed his head.

"What really saddened me was that this wasn't just one or two punks—this was a fairly large group of fairly nicely dressed kids," said Larry later. "What if the rock that cut my back had hit my head? What if I'd have fallen? What if..."

Now it would be easy to say that the people who threw rocks at Larry are 'animals', and should be treated as such—but they are not. They are our children. The collective children of St. John. They are us.

We are all only human; we are all the parents of our society. When our children do good, we are proud of them. We bask in their reflective glory. This is natural; this is normal. And when our children do evil, we are all diminished. Shamed. Lessened.

The rock that hit Larry knocked out some of the love, admiration, and respect he was developing for the people of this community. That rock also knocked away some of the heart-felt pride I have for my beloved island home. That rock slapped every caring, decent, law-abiding St. John citizen in the face. It made a mockery of our internal self-image, the words of our leaders, the daily lessons of our school teachers, the lyrics of our songs, and the writings of our poets. Cruz Bay isn't Love City anymore.

And, yes, I haven't forgotten this is a marine column. A few days after this incident I was chatting with some marine industry leaders and governmental officials, and they asked me what we should do to regain our position as the #1 chartering destination in the Caribbean. I kept saying, "I don't know, I don't know," but was thinking "How can we stop our youngsters from throwing stones at one another? At others? At their own future?"

Larry Best at the wheel of *Osprey*

Sint Maarten's Multi Madness

The island of Sint Maarten/St. Martin has two names because it has two distinct personalities, two national flags, and two different lifestyles. Half Dutch and half French—this borderless laid-back tropical island combines the best of both cultures with a calypso beat. Located just 100 miles to the east of the Virgins on the Nor'east corner of the Lesser Antilles, Sint Maarten/St. Martin is surrounded by Anguilla, St. Barts, St. Kitts, Statia, and Saba. The Dutch population is an industrious 30,000, while the French side has an artful 20,000 souls.

The marine community of the 35 square mile emerald isle is truly a diverse one, and numerous sailors from Holland, France, South Africa, England, America, and Australia have 'swallowed the hook' here.

About the only thing they—and their many Caribbean neighbors agree on—is that Sint Maarten/St. Martin is the multihull capital of the Eastern Caribbean. There are a number of delightful reasons why this is so.

First and foremost was an innovative, opinionated, out-spoken Dutchman from South Africa by the name of Peter Spronk. It was his genius, hard work, creativity, entrepreneurial drive, and force of personality which were directly responsible for his island's original interest in modern multihulls. He was the right man in the right place at the right time.

Back in the 1960s, he started building large wooden sailing catamarans in the Simpson Bay Lagoon area. His designs were stylish, practical, sea-worthy, economical, and very well-engineered. They were specifically designed for the local waters, with low cross beams, low split rigs, minimum freeboard, thin V lapstrake hulls with fine ends, and slender daggerboards. They possessed both tremendous speed and great structural strength, and were an instant local success.

His local boat building crew was fiercely devoted to Spronk and his philosophy, and lovingly constructed his elegantly designed vessels to the highest of yacht standards. The boats soon attracted both world-wide attention and admiration. Orders flooded in, and he was soon able to concentrate on projects which especially interested him.

Spronk was not only a designer, engineer, and builder—he was also a visionary. He birthed each new design as if it was his last, and slaved away over the drawing board endlessly in search of the 'perfect' catamaran.

Of course, he never obtained his goal, but he *did* manage to pass along some of the fire in his belly to a new, eager generation of Sint Maarten boat builders.

Dozens of the shipwrights (disciples) Spronk trained eventually went on to design and built their own multihull craft. Each new design spurred on another, and then another. A certain synergy began to take place. (In St. Croix, a fellow named Dick Newick triggered an almost identical explosion of multihull interest during the same time span. Cruzian Roger Hatfield & Gold Coast Yachts now carry on his tradition.)

Peter Spronk designed, engineered, and constructed wonderfully fast, stable catamaran 'platforms' which were (by design) ideally suited for local conditions. They could stand up to 20+ knots dead-on-the-nose forever, and yet were also superb performers while spinnaker reaching in the brisk nor'east tradewinds.

Soon a fellow leased one of Spronk's boats, and started carrying 'day-trippers' between Dutch Sint Maarten and French St. Barts twenty miles away. Almost overnight, the Spronk 'cattle-marans' became solid money-makers.

Just as the rest of the world was turning its back on carrying passengers for hire under sail—a number of Spronk cats were specifically designed and built to do exactly that. The geography, wind, and weather conditions between Sint Maarten and St. Barts were ideal for these large catamarans. They could carry a large number of people in safety and comfort at relatively fast speeds. And they were very economical to operate. (Yes, the wind is still free!)

Sint Maarten was suddenly blessed with two new industries on its shores—
multihull boat building and daysail chartering to St. Barts.

Of course, there was a French influence. The French are certainly the fastest, most innovative multihull sailors in the world, and much of their enthusiasm for the concept rubbed off on the local builders. Technology from France, England, America, and the South Pacific all filtered into Sint Maarten via globe-trotting multihull sailors cruising through. The Gougeon Brothers in Bay City, Michigan suddenly began shipping large amounts of WEST™ epoxy to the Eastern Caribbean.

Then a guy named Dougie Brookes, a former foreman at Spronk's yard, started building cats on nearby St. Kitts. One of his early boats was a lean, mean ocean racing catamaran named *Spirit of St. Kitts*, and it impressed all the multihull sailors of Europe in such events as the Around Britain race and many other international racing events.

The proverbial 'cat' was out of the bag—the Sint Maarten and St. Kitts area was producing some of the highest tech (yet basically simple) catamarans in the world.

Dougie Brooks then designed and built such catamarans as *Falcon*, *Eagle*, *Indigo*, and many others. (Brookes wife, Evelyn, eventually took over the management of *Eagle* in the St. Bart's run.) When Peter

Spronk finally moved off Sint Maarten to Grenada, Dougie Brookes became the new Guru of Glue in the Eastern Caribbean.

The more the boats made money carrying passengers, the more 'cattle-marans' were built. More and more visitors sailed on them to St. Barts, and experienced first hand their many advantages as stable passenger carriers. Even tradition-bound monohull sailors began to begrudgingly afford them some respect.

A little mini-culture sprung up among the St. Barts cats and their trendy, lively crews. They had their own heros, legends, and stories. They were a culture within a culture within a culture. They were notorious partiers and bon vivants. They kissed life full on the lips, and danced daily on both foredecks and dance floors. To boogie with these boys and girls was to boogie with the best.

A skipper named David Crowley steered a Spronk cat named *El Tigre* back and forth to St. Barts for over ten years without ever injuring a passenger or having a serious mechanical problem with the boat. (He reportedly sailed a distance of 2 ½ times around the world on *El Tigre!*)

Many newcomers who sailed into Sint Maarten aboard cruising sailboats got their first 'shore' jobs in the local marine industry aboard one of these cats. Many of them fell in love with both Sint Maarten and multihull sailing at the same time. A surprising number have stayed, and are currently working in the construction, tourism, and marine trades.

Of course, with all those sailing craft plying the waters between Sint Maarten and St. Barts—they raced. At first it was just informal 'pick-up' races, and then later they entered such organized events as the Heineken regatta.

Racing—especially racing these large, fast, highly engineered exotic craft—is stressful on both boat and crew. A five dollar piece of gear failing can bring down a $40,000 mast in the blink of an eye—and often does. A tiny mistake in judgement can cost a small fortune. ("Anybody who buys a boat with two hulls, and then spends the rest of their life attempting to sail it on one—*has* to be nuts!")

But the racing of boats, just like the racing of cars or planes, is the quickest way to ensure their speedy evolution. In order to correctly engineer boats which *won't* break you have to have some idea *when* and *how* they *will* break. Racing is, perhaps, a crude method of achieving this worthy goal, but also probably the most practical.

Of course, racing vessels flat-out on Sunday that are supposed to be sedately carrying passengers for profit on Monday makes little rational sense. But that has traditionally been a large part of the Sint Maarten multihull mystique. Call it 'multihull madness' if you will, but racing has been an integral part of the Philipsburg 'multi-style' for decades.

During the 1992 12th Annual Heineken regatta, the Dougie Brookes-designed, Evelyn Brookes-owned 70 foot *Eagle* flipped over while spinnaker-reaching in 25+ knots of wind. She was reported to be going nearly 30 knots when she went over.

Owner Evelyn Brookes admitted at the time, "Hey, maybe this racing business isn't such a good idea, eh?"

But for the hardworking men and women who design, engineer, and build these giant cats—the boats are far more than mere daysail boats. They are a Way of Life. To their salt-stained, go-for-it sailing crews, the boats aren't merely multi-passenger transportational devices. They are their communal life-styles, their professions, their hobbies, their recreation, and even their sport's competition. Their individual pride, honor, love, and self-respect are hopelessly intertwined with their specific craft. That's why they take such good care of the boats, fly their respective colors so proudly, and continuously sing their vessel's praises.

And that's also why the rest of the Caribbean marine sailing community cheers them on at the finish line, and sheds a genuine tear of sorrow when one breaks or 'crashes and burns' as it flips over. They are—for better or worse—our hallowed high-speed harbor heros. And ultimately it isn't really important which vessel wins or loses—only that they played the game to the best of their ability.

Sint Maarten/St. Martin—two countries sharing a single island uniquely perched on the cutting edge of international multi-madness!

Caribbean Latitudes and Attitudes

Back in the '70s —a refugee from the '60s—I sailed into the
Caribbean Sea. Like so many of my generation, I was restless, and
driven, and disillusioned. While many of my friends 'returned to the
farm', I sought a change in attitude through a change in latitude. The
Lesser Antilles seemed a sunny place for shady people. I fled
southward.

The passage was rough; a thousand ocean miles dead into the teeth
of the Trades. I brought with me a rude boat carved by my own hand, a
strong woman I wanted to share my life with—and not much else.

When we were finally able to ease sheets, we came roaring into
Drake's Passage in the Virgins. The air was suddenly laced with the
sweet, fruity scent of tropical flowers. The island of Tortola slid by to
loo'ard—impossibly lush and green and mysterious. Coconut palms
appeared to be waving welcome. Ripe papaya, mango, and breadfruit
trees seemed to dance along the shores. Waves splashed diamonds on
the beaches. Fields of bananas wiggled in the glinting sun.

Within that single moment of vivid memory—like a color slide
plucked from a stack of black-and-white prints—I was forever changed.
The next few months of cruising confirmed it. My past life seemed
mere preparation—with the immediate future as exciting as a tropical
promise whispered by a sea shell. I suddenly wanted to kiss my
existence full on the lips, without restraint or care. My mid-latitude
attitudes gradually shifted, and I was (once again) able to laugh like a
child. For the first time as an adult I was happy where I was. My eternal
quest for the horizon was over, at least for awhile.

Picture God's hands cupped into the most benign section of the
Atlantics. A pool of fathomless blue, with His palms as South and
Central America, and His fingertips as the Greater Antilles (Cuba,
Hispaniola, Puerto Rico) and the Lesser Antilles— from the Virgins
southward to Trinidad. Add the Nor'east Tradewinds—the mighty sun-
kissed engine of it all. Color in the waters—from the clearest of whites
to the palest of greens to the most eternal of deep, deep blues. Accept
the jagged improbability of the jutting verdant islands of stone and rock
and coral and tree— how lofty and solid and safe they squat upon the
lapping sea.

She is a study in contrasts, this one million square mile mini-ocean;
ever-changing yet always the same. Tranquil in her normal sleepy-eyed
slumbers; she can become utterly savage in the blink of a hurricane's
eye. She is noted for her peacefulness, and yet she is unmistakably
untamed/wild/primitive.

Her written history is one of idiocy. Cold white men in far-away places slashed at their treaties and contracts with mercilessly sharp pens—and the scuppers of their tropical sailing ships ran red with blood 4,000 miles away.

Cannons, sugar cane, and rum barrels soon dotted the shore. Pirates and missionaries and businessmen carved up the waterfront. Great cities were built even as their sponsoring empires crumbled. The harsh realities of the international marketplace rapidly showed all men—black, red, brown, and white—that the color of their blood, sweat, and tears were indistinguishable under a tropical sun.

Diversity? The Caribbean is as diverse as the peaceful Arawak Indians and fierce Caribe Indians of South America—as sophisticated as the ancient Mayans—as culturally rich as England, France, Spain, Portugal, Sweden, and Holland. Currently, the East Indian population on certain islands is growing nearly as fast as its West Indian one. The growing live-aboard sailing community ("We're all her because we're not all there!") is primarily American, with a rich mix of European sailors drifting in from the east.

Throughout it all, of course, weaves the African. It is his culture—his music, his art, his dance — which permeates the Caribbean. His sun-washed smile, his elastic sense of time, his concept of family/tribe/community sets the tone.

The poetry of Bob Marley, the literature of V.S. Naipal, the paintings of Haiti, those steel drums, that Calypsonian saying—are all fruits of the Caribbean Experience.

Luckily, the equatorial sun eventually bleaches out everything—even the stain of slavery.

People of Color are the majority in most Caribbean Nations—and many of the most contented, most efficient, most prosperous islands are governed by a polyglot group of folks who have long ago ceased to care about the past political divisions of the bloodlines of their neighbor.

Boat builders are more revered than lawyers; a fella who can catch fish is everybody's friend. A good outboard mechanic can become King—but would have to take a cut in pay.

Life isn't necessarily less complex here—island society is quite sophisticated and subtle—but it *is* more in tune with its people. Harmony in the Caribbean isn't limited to church choirs. It is difficult to get angry when everything is OK, and has been for a long time, and probably always will be.

There is no reason to rush, to worry, or to get uptight. Relax. Do it later. Tomorrow will be just as perfect. "Doan vex yourself, Mon..." is a common West Indian saying.

By any measure, this mini-ocean is a wonderful place. But it is especially blessed for the cruising sailor—as if God, Walt Disney, and

Joshua Slocum consulted to make a heaven on earth for sailors.

Most islands in the Lesser Antilles are a mere daysail away from one another. You can sail from Dutch Sint Maarten down the Lesser Antilles chain to Venezuela and *back*—all without ever being hard on the wind. The Trades blow from the East at 16 to 20 knots, and have since the beginning of recorded history. It rarely rains, and you need an accurate thermometer to tell winter from summer. The water is deep, the harbors plentiful, and the one navigation rule is "Doan mash dey mountain, Mon!"

'Perfect' seems too weak a superlative.

The real miracle of the Caribbean is—that it exists. I, too, used to think that it was a figment of men's imaginations, trick photography, an adult fairy tale spoon-fed to the winter weary. No more.

The truth is that she is waiting right now—only a sailboat ride, an airplane ticket, an ocean liner, or a tramp steamer passage away. Anyone with a lustful sense of adventure can take her hand, succumb to her easy island rhythms, dive into her warm, water-colored embrace. It is as easy as falling asleep at the beach. The love affair can last for a week's charter, a year's cruise, or, in my case, a lifetime.

I'm still not jaded—despite the thousands of sea-miles we've sailed in the Caribbean over the last decade. Our charts are tattered, torn, and spider-webbed with faded courses. No matter. It is still fun—the wind is still free. Within a few days we'll be setting sail for St. Barths—a formerly Swedish island now operating with a French accent. Nice place—rather 'trendy' right now—but still a Sunny Place for Shady People.

Fast Eddie of St. Barths, FWI

YOU GOTTA REGATTA

Trimaran *Alien* with some of her crew; Jody, Scooter, Kay, and Captain Joe

The Savage Realities of an *"Alien"* Encounter

Joe Colpitt is a soft-spoken, mild-mannered, laid-back, low-key kind of guy. His response to Life-As-Most-People-Know-It is often a bemused, slightly puzzled shrug. His favorite statement is a tentative, "Well..." trailing off into cosmic nothingness. Nothing ever rattles Joe. He's cool as a cucumber. Serene. Quiet. Unobtrusive.

But that's only part of the story—only one side of his remarkable character. Also within the soul of Joe lurks a balls-to-the-wall salt-stained sailing adventurer. He 'gets off' by repeatedly racing exotic, fragile multihulls across lonely stretches of rough oceans. He builds the state-of-the-art radical multihull vessels with his own calloused hands—then pushes them to within a few pounds of their absolute design limits— while his own life hangs in the balance.

Yeah, as sailors go, Joe is the Ultimate Gambler. (Timothy

McKegney, famed skipper of the radical trimaran *Adrenalin*, once summed up all offshore multihull racers in two short words. "Sick puppies!")

Besides building and racing multihulls, Joe likes to read. He's a Sci-Fi nut—a Stranger in a Strange Land. His nose is always in a thick book. Joe's never been quite comfortable on this planet. Perhaps that why he built his latest 40 foot 'spaceship' of a trimaran and named it *Alien*.

Oh. One other thing. Joe likes to have fun. Lots of it.

That was his downfall, of course. He cruised into St. John many years back, and soon got hooked up with the Infamous Monkey Crew of Cruz Bay. He took Jody Culbert (*Foxfire*) along on the Carlsberg Two Star Trans-Atlantic race—and managed to beat everything under 60 feet! He wiped Scooter Mejia off the bar ("Hard aground again on the Mahogany reef!") at the Back Yard Bar on St. John— and soon had him screaming along the coast of South America at over 20 knots...

...and so when Joe decided to race in the 12th Annual STYC/STXYC Memorial Day race... he decided to take the 'Biggest Risk Possible' with his crew list.

That's right! Despite all advice, all common sense, all logic—despite repeated dire warnings of the havoc which would surely result—Joe Colpitt invited Cap'n Fatty himself to sail aboard *Alien*.

It was an offer—needless to say—I couldn't refuse.

It was, truly, a 'Crew List Made in Hell.' Joe would steer, and act as sailing master. Jody agreed to call tactics—despite later admitting he had no real idea of what a tactic was, or what to do with one should he stumble across it by random chance... Scooter signed on to run the foredeck...

...and I solemnly agreed to take charge of the beer cooler. "No matter what happens out there," I promised grimly, "we'll have the proper drinks for it. It's important; and besides, it's my job. You can count on me!!!"

It seemed to reassure them.

Since most American girls are far too smart to act as a Bilge Bunny to the Monkey Crew's Multi Division—as usual, we had to settle for a foreign gal just passing through. Kay was from Scotland, kept urging us (between hiccups) to 'get into' kilts, and knew how to say, "Hey, Jimmy, buy me a drink?" in 23 languages. She rounded out the crew quite nicely.

We raced over from St. Thomas to St Croix, and despite leaving an hour later than the monohulls, we couldn't even see their sails astern as we came swooping down on St. Croix (3 hrs 10 mins).

Of course, the committee boat wasn't quite in place, and we had some sadistic fun sailing faster than the committee boat could power as it attempted to both set the mark and avoid being run down by us...

But the race over there wasn't important. We knew we could beat a bunch of stone-age monohulls. ("Sea Slugs!") After all, monohulls pretty much stopped evolving back in the cavemen days. They move faster than glaciers—but not by much. (The idea of carrying around large chunks of dense lead suspended below a vessel's hull *does* seem a tad insane...)

What we were after was the Buck Island Boys—and the famous Roger Hatfield of Gold Coast Marine.

After terrorizing the committee boat for awhile (picture American Christian Pioneers besieged by a wild group of rampaging Indians on go-carts, and you'll get the idea...), we sheered off for Buck Island. All the hot cats and tris in the St. Croix day-sail game were sailing back after a day of fun in the sun. We keep swinging up alongside, and shouting 'You're dead meat tomorrow! DEAD MEAT!!!" at their skippers. (Some of their guests burst into tears at our crude threats—but tourists are often notoriously thin-skinned...)

After verbally harassing the Buck Island Boys, we reached off into the St. Croix Yacht Club—and promptly lay siege to the bar. Luckily a former St. Johnian named Vicky Brown was tending bar at the Yacht Club, and she knew how quickly we could get ugly if our alcohol flow was interrupted even briefly. There was no problem—it was two for us, and one for everyone else.

It was a good thing, too. Tomorrow we'd face some of the hottest cats and tris in the Caribbean. We certainly weren't going to attempt such a sick trick without a severe, brain-crushing hangover!

We stayed at the bar during the skipper's meeting. We heard a lot of talk about 'gates'—but we were already inside the yacht club... so, what did we care about what was happening to those poor souls outside beyond the gates..?

Before crashing out, there was one more task we had to accomplish. We roamed the harbor, waving our wicked rigging knives, and bluntly begging spinnakers with the dreaded line, "Your chute, or your life!!!"

It worked. Two different people decided that their lives were far more valuable than their spinnakers. "Please return... what's ever left..." said one of the fellows who knew us well. We snarled our agreement.

At the start of the multihull class on Sunday, the tension aboard *Alien* was extreme. Joe had recently spend a lot of time, talent, and money building *Alien* in Brazil, and was finally getting her 'dialed in' to the proper 'numbers'. She was half-way 'up-to-speed' towards her potential performance. The question was simply this: how would she do against *Teroro* and Roger Hatfield's famed *Hatter*—two fast trimarans well-sailed by two experienced racers?

The time for talk was over. It was 'put up, or shut up' time. Reality.

We were too early approaching the line at the start, and had to 'round down' and gybe for another pass. Monohulls scattered like leaves in the wind as we unexpectedly turned towards them at 18 knots. ("It's like a scary video game—but with real boats!" somebody laughed.)

Teroro was first over the line, with good boat speed. We limped over, while Roger Hatfield on *Hatter* came over third.

Ten minutes later, *Hatter* passed us on our windward side—and we were a glum group. He was pointing higher and footing just as fast. Both our arch rivals were now ahead. Since they were intimately familiar with the local waters—we followed them. We wallowing in their wake and bad air loathing every second of it. Finally we decided 'to hell with it'—and tacked away. Joe started sailing his boat fast—without thought to our competitors tacking angles or boat speed.

Each time we'd cross tacks, we'd gain a little.

It was sort of exciting. (I admit, I was having a little trouble controlling my bladder during all this high speed excitement...)

Half way to the weather mark, we passed *Teroro*.

Only *Hatter* stood in our way. "We're gonna get 'em," I was chanting. "We're gonna get 'em! We're gonna eat 'em up. He's dead meat. He's DEAD MEAT!!!"

At the windward mark, *Hatter* came screaming in from the north, as we came roaring up from the south. "Starboard!!!" we yelled at the top of our collective lungs.

We rounded ahead. Our spinnaker work was horribly sloppy; his was even worse. We started pulling away, and kept pulling away even after his spinnaker set.

Then the chute blew up on us—shredded its self into a million ribbons—and *Hatter* and *Teroro* were coming back strong as we rounded the reaching mark.

We got a few of the larger pieces of the chute back aboard, and rehoisted our jib. ("Thank gosh we borrowed two chutes," somebody said. "Yeah," said another. "And wait until I get my hands on the creep that attempted to foist off a defective sail on us!!! That's... that's *criminal!*")

Heading back to windward it was *Alien* clearly in the lead, with *Teroro* second, and *Hatter* third.

Suddenly, *Hatter* peeled off, and headed for the unfavored side of the course. We debated if Roger Hatfield was attempting to get out of the current, catch a windshift, etc—just what the hell was Ole Roger doing, anyway...

...but *Teroro* was pressing us too hard for us give it much thought. We concentrated on boat speed, and gradually pulled up to windward.

On the down wind leg to the finish line, we blew the other chute. It dropped right in the water dead ahead of us, and spun us around as we sailed directly into it at 16+ knots. "Wham!" It got caught on our centerboard, and twisted up in our rudder. We were dead in the water. It was a big mess, and required many loud swear words to wrestle under control.

It cost us time, and turned our cake-walk finish into a horse race with *Teroro*. Roger Hatfield was way back there...

We crossed the finish line while loudly congratulating ourselves about our solid victory. "We won! We did it! DEAD MEAT! We aced it..! VICTORY AND VINDICATION!!!"

I looked at the committee boat. They didn't give us a gun—not even a horn. Their eyes were averted, for the most part, and those that did glance our way did so out of pity.

"Oophs," I said. "Something's wrong. I think we're about to snatch defeat from the jaws of victory..."

Teroro crossed the line—and also was greeted with silence.

Hatter finally came in, and got the gun.

It was then that we decided—that maybe, just maybe—we should read the race instructions. They clearly stated that we were supposed to go through two sets of 'gates' on the final windward leg; we'd only gone through one set. We were dead wrong, and all realized it at the same instant. Instead of earning line honors, and being first in class—we'd earned a DSQ, and become the laughing-stock of the Caribbean!

"Oh, gosh," wept Scooter as he read the race instructions aloud. "We can sail fast but its obvious we're *way* too dumb to win..."

We entered the Yacht Club singing the chorus of a song from the Wizard of Oz... "...if we only had a brain..!"

Ever the journalist, I asked Joe how he felt about it.

"Well..." he said, so softly I could barely hear. "I don't think I really want to talk about it..."

That evening, we partied/hearty with Roger Hatfield and numerous other "multi-freaks" of St. Croix. Jody told Roger, "If we knew you were going to read the race instructions—understand the—and even follow them intelligently... we'd have never even *attempted* to beat you!!!"

For the next day's race back to St. Thomas, we took John Holmberg aboard—and placed him in charge of everything. It didn't seem possible we could have screwed up the course, but we weren't taking any dumb chances.

All the way across we kept saying things like, "I can't *believe* we blew it!"

Scooter kept muttering the Monkey Crew motto: "What we lack in intelligence, we more than make up for in velocity!!!"

"Now," somebody said, "if we could only learn how to read!!!"

Alien zooming along with full racing sails

'Blue Shirt' Sails On *'De Tree '*

I was extremely nervous standing there on the blazing beach in the hot sun—it was less than a minute away from the start of the race. Captain Eroll Romney, a living legend in the Leeward Islands, was perched on the transom of his new traditional Anguillan racing sloop named *De Tree*. He seemed to be avoiding my eyes as he scanned the sizzling beach of Sandy Ground for his missing crew member.

"Damn it," I whispered to myself, "I'm not going to make it. I'm gonna be left on the beach *again,* just like last year and the year before that..."

Then Captain Romney looked me straight in the eye, as if he was measuring me. He gave a slight nod of acceptance, and then glanced away. I experienced a nano-second of self-doubt, and then found myself wildly sprinting down the beach, splashing through the waist-deep water, and swan-diving ungracefully over the rail into *De Tree*.

Yes, I was finally going to realize a long cherished dream—to race aboard a traditional Anguillan racing sloop during their annual August Monday series.   About twenty seconds before the starting gun, the roar of the assembled crowd and excited boat crews drowned out all other sounds of carnival. All twelve of the Class A 28 foot wooden sloops were turned downwind, pointing away from the beach. This required four or five of their largest crew members in the water to hold the boat, in addition to a stout line to shore. Even so, the boats were difficult to contain.

Their massive mainsails filled and shook and rattled. From stem to stern—from keel to masthead—they quivered like excited horses straining to be off.

Boat race committee chairmen Harris Richardson, his white beard leaping off a black face permanently creased into a wide smile, was just down from us on the sun-scorched beach. He was yelling something, waving his arms. Suddenly a starter's pistol appeared in his massive hand. "Bang!"

All twelve of the wooden boats literally leapt away from the beach. Our forty foot long wooden boom raked the entire length of the vessel on our starboard side. To our port, two vessels were jammed hopelessly together, as if wrestling. A number of boats were forced to leave members of their crew behind in the water. We managed to claw all four of our crew back aboard with much swearing, yelling, and butt-yanking.

The acceleration was incredible. It was neck-snapping. I felt like I was on a high-tech multihull, not a traditional Caribbean sailing craft.

God, we were moving. The trade winds were fresh, and we were carrying about a thousand square feet of sail dead down wind. I couldn't wipe the smile off my face.

"Blue shirt, blue shirt!" the mate roared. "Move it up, mon! Feel de boat, feel the boat!"

At first I didn't realize he was speaking to me. Somebody gave me a gentle nudge, and I moved forward as trim ballast. Then I realized I had just gotten my Anguillan sailing name. The only white boy within a couple of nautical miles was now officially named 'Blue Shirt'.

"Work the boat! Work the boat!" someone was shouting. Our 'jib mon' was acting as a human whisker pole as we sped downwind (wing & wing) with a bone in our teeth for Dog Rocks. "Blue shirt! Come back a little... more... dat good! Down de road, mon, down de road she go!"

I glanced aft at Captain Eroll Romney. He was far down inside the hull, only his head and large tiller hand was sticking above the sheerline. A huge barefoot was resting on the mainsheet bight, ready to instantly release should there be a sudden gust.

There was a look of intense concentration on Captain Romney's face; a blissful, boyish, expectant look.

"Fresh up! Fresh up!" cried out a young kid on the starboard rail. "She get plenty wind soon, mon! Plenty wind..."

The gust hit us, and shook the boat like a rag in a dog's mouth. *De Tree* staggered drunkenly for a moment, and then shot off down wind like a scalded cat. Our bow wave was so big, I was scared we were going to just sail her underwater, pitch-pole her. I flashed on last weekend's race, when five of the boats sank, leaving sixty men in the water...

"Scrape her! Scrape her..!" We were taking a lot of water over the loo'ard rail as our bow dipped and curtsied to the swells. The white frothing foam of our bow wave was constantly slopping aboard.

A young kid grabbed an old Clorox bottle with the bottom cut out and started 'scraping' the bilge water over the side.

Then a breaking rock off Dog Island was just over our bows. "Ready... ready... NOW!" said the mate as we hardened up to windward.

It took three large men to honk in the mainsheet. When the forty foot boom was almost centerlined, it had almost a four foot bend in it. I thought it would snap at any moment. It took two men to wrestle the clew of the jib down, and a boy to tie it off around a ribband.

While this was happening, about ten of the crew were hiking out on the windward rail. The 'pig iron man' shifted three giant cast iron ballast pieces to the windward side. He was careful to set them spanning frames—if dropped on the planks, they might go right through. Meanwhile, the 'sand man' also lugged a two hundred pound burlap sack of sand up the windward side as well.

The wind slackened for a moment. "Inside! Inside" was the call as we shifted inward. We moved back outwards as the wind filled in. "Outside! Feel de boat, feel de boat..."

Our first tack was fairly smooth. "Okay," said the skipper as he pushed the tiller to leeward. We slowly and carefully moved as a group from one side of the boat to the other, careful not to heel her on the other tack too fast. There was somewhat of a bottle neck as a dozen men tried to move around the pig iron man and the sand man.

We had only squared away on our new tack for a few moments when we were hailed with a frantic "Hard Lee!" from another boat. I only had a brief moment to stick my head above the rail to see the other vessel charging at our side.

Our ensuing crash tack was bedlam. Some of the crew shifted too fast. I attempted to stay in the middle, but the pig-iron man backed into me. I went down, hard. My foot jammed between a frame, plank, and ribband. I felt a sharp pain. A two hundred pound sack of sand thudded into my right shoulder. Somebody stepped on my stomach, and I felt the air 'whoosh' out of me. A piece of wire or an exposed nail was grinding into my back.

There was much swearing and yelling. When we finally got all squared away, many of our crew were bleeding from wounds both minor and major.

I had a scraped right elbow, a jagged cut on my left arm, and a bruised collar bone. I couldn't tell how bad the puncture wound was on my back.

This was the first time I'd ever thought of yacht racing as a contact sport. I'd come through Chicago gang fights with less damage...

We were half way to Island Harbour when we were forced by another 'hard lee' situation to sail in amid the reefs. I knew we were doing something truly dangerous when the entire boat got suddenly quiet. Normally the crew chatter continuously, mostly about how amazingly skillful the island women were in the varied arts of love —but now you could hear a pin drop.

I stuck my sweating head up, and peered over the starboard side. An awash coral head scooted by not ten feet from the boat. Another lay just fifty feet ahead. "Down, down, down!" Somebody was shouting to the skipper. "Down *now!*"

Another person recommended the opposite. "Tack! Tack!"

Many of us seemed frozen. Time slowed. The coral head seemed to glide towards us in freeze-frame. Captain Romney craned his neck this way and that—searching for an escape. Suddenly, he shot the eye of the wind. Just before the boat lost all weigh and was thrown into irons—he forced her bow down to her original course. He had neither tacked nor fallen off—and he'd brought her through the sea of coral heads as fast as possible.

I gasped for air, not realizing that I'd been holding my breath during the entire maneuver. "Up de road, up the road," someone sang out—and we were all back hiking on the rail, hunting for the next boat to overtake.

We spotted the finishing buoy just off Island Harbour about a half hour later. (There was no finish line, you had to physically touch the finishing buoy.)

For awhile we were hopeful of finishing 'in the money' at fourth place or better —but as it became apparent that we were going to be fifth out of twelve boats we twisted away. "It doan't matter after four," someone said. "Only de first four count..."

Immediately, the race was forgotten. The talk turned to women, boats, and drinking—as it does anywhere in the world where fifteen horny sailor men with lots of callouses come together. As soon as we came ashore, I marched across the beach into Johnno's Bar to find a bottle of Mount Gay to hug. I was leaking blood from a couple of places, but I didn't care. It was, I admit, difficult not to swagger.

Traditional island sloops often compete in local races like the one pictured here in Carriacou.

Grumpy's Gruesome Regatta

When I first heard that some brain-dead sailor-geeks on St. John were planning to revive the infamous *You-Gotta-Gotta-Regatta*... well, frankly, I was horrified.

I happen to be one of the few survivors of that weird & twisted event, and I'm still licking my scars—physically, metaphysically, and psychologically.

It was back in the mid-80s, I remember that much.

This was before most of my friends went to jail, de-tox, or heaven. Yeah, a long, long time ago. Before I got Al What's-His-Name disease.

Anyway, that original race was sponsored by a particularly ugly group of varnish-sniffing yacht-Nazis who called themselves the *Virgin Islands Snot Club (VISC)*.

(The above paragraph may strike some people as a little harsh, but *trust me...* I'm being as kind and up-beat as I possibly can.)

The regatta itself was a pretty gruesome event. Picture a yacht race organized by Charlie Manson, Dennis-Conner-on-downers, and Tom Waits—and you're close to the disgusting reality of it. (There were extra points for *dwarf-tossing,* for gosh sakes!) This wasn't a GP, family-type, wholesome sailing event. It was a XXX, hard-core, salt-stained, floating-flesh-fetish kind of scene.

During the final '2nd Last Annual' *You-Gotta-Gotta-Regatta* there were almost as many collisions as entries. One boat dismasted; another sunk. The committee boat was taken over by 64 sun-crazed nudists. About 25 marriages ended. Lots of people forgot who they were; a few never remembered.

So when I heard that the *You-Gotta-Gotta-Regatta* might be reincarnated as the *You-Gotta-Colada-Regatta*... I had to immediately find out if it was true. So I quickly set off to find live-aboard sailor Tumbling Tom of Great Cruz Bay, another veteran-of-vice from the previous regatta.

Now Tumbling Tom is an institution on St. John (or should be institutionalized, I'm not sure which). Anyway, Tumbling Tom got his name because he frequently falls down, no matter how nicely they prop him up. He started out falling off commercial buildings as a kid, then residential roofs as a young man, and has finally worked his way down to bar stools in his middle age.

I found Tumbling Tom at the bar at *Grumpy's Almost-By-the-Sea.* (It would be *By-the-Sea* if it or the sea were in a different place!) "Ahoy Tom!" I shouted at him.

Perhaps I'd shouted too loudly—his entire body spasmed as if a cattle prod had just whacked a particularly sensitive area of his prostrate. Luckily I was ready, and caught him in my arms as he pole-axed backwards off the bar stool.

"Fatty! FATTY!" He sputtered as I hoisted him back onto his perch. "Don't *do* that to me..!"

"I need information," I told him briskly. "So I came to you for the straight scoop.."

"You can depend on me for the straight poop... er, I mean scoop," he said.

I could tell he was serious when he put his beer out in his ashtray, and took a drink from his cigarette.

I looked around the gritty interior of Grumpy's Bar and Restaurant. It was mostly dim and dusty—a great place to grow mushrooms, weave spider webs, and ride 'mahogany birds' bare-back. The bar itself had obviously been fist-banged and drool-hugged by every rum-laced sailor in the Caribbean.

It was fairly crowded at the time I was there, but only a few of the patrons appeared to be actually alive. The sign in front said something about 'hang-overs and hurricanes', and I was wondering how many of its patrons would be able to tell the difference.

"Rumor has it that another twisted and sick regatta is being planned," I said to Tumbling Tom out of the corner of my mouth. "Is there any truth to it?"

"Truth?" Tom blanched, his blood-shot eyes suddenly hemorrhaging little red mini-flares of distress. "You came to me for TRUTH!"

Obviously, I'd insulted him—and hit a sore spot smack dab in the middle of his flabby, festering paranoia. "Chill, Tom, chill!" I ordered. "Just point me in the right direction..."

Tom hooked a thumb towards the back of the bar, and I caught the slo-mo glint of a dull eye peering through some heavy, acrid smoke.

I realized (with a certain amount of dread) that what I thought was a small kitchen fire in the back room was actually Grumpy himself smoking a fat cigar.

Now this Grumpy fella is a piece of work, I'll tell you. At best, he looks sorta like a Buddha-Gone-Real-Bad. At worse, he looks... well, worse. He's a large, bathroom-scale-crushing sort of fellow—with a mind as fast as molasses.

Now there are two distinct schools of thought on Grumpy. One camp says that he is a grumpy-guy-with-a-heart-of-gold, and the other camp says that he is just a grumpy guy.

I personally haven't quite decided which camp is more accurate, but I tend to agreed that both are at least *partially* correct.

"Are you sponsoring this new regatta," I asked him point-blank.

There was a long pause (long even by St. John standards), and then he nodded oh-so-slowly in the affirmative.

"When?" I asked, attempting to hide my personal repugnance at the whole idea.

"Couple of weeks," he said tentatively. "More or less. About. Around. Maybe."

Now my first idea, naturally, was to grab the wife and kid—and flee the island that week end. That would certainly be the safe, wise, and sensible thing to do. No one would blame me—nobody remotely sane, that is.

However, I am—first and foremost—a professional inkslinger. *Caribbean Boating* has been depending on me for over ten years now to bring them as much marine-related filth and cheap sensationalism as possible—and I didn't want to let them down. After all, I didn't get to be the least-respected-yacht-journalist-ever by covering the easy PHRF-type stuff. No sirree! These were my people, and I was their Boswel—no matter how depressing that may be for both of us.

Thus, in the end I decided to (once again!) put my liver on the line for yachting.

To describe the skipper's meeting as 'total bedlam' is to offer it more decorum than it deserved. A frizzy-haired blond guy named Robbie was yelling out the course instructions—his shrill voice was completely drowned out by the fiery sounds of Grumpy's bulging cash register melting down. Neil Newhart tossed random PHRF ratings into the crowd like confetti. Some crazy red-haired chick from Minneapolis was *already* attempting to get naked.

The crowd was the usual mix of outrageous out-patients from San Quinten, Bellevue, and the Betty Ford Clinic. Almost everyone had a parrot—they wouldn't even let you in the door unless *something* had defecated on your shoulder. The only guy there without a gold earring was *gay!* A number of guys *looked* like salty-seadogs; an even greater number *smelled* like them!

The official title of the race was *GRUMPY'S 1st Annual Samurai Seavent You Gotta Colada Regatta.* (Catchy, huh?) It was sponsored locally by Don Q Rum, and the entire entry fee went straight to the St. Jude's Children's Hospital. (Okay, okay... score a point for the heart-of-gold group!)

The actual race itself was made as confusing as possible. It was a 'timed start' based on a (slightly bent) PHRF rating, and went from Cruz Bay to Congo (S) to Whistling Cay (S) to Two Brothers (P) to Stevens Cay (P) to a finish off Cruz Bay.

The racing instructions were a tad bizarre. They mentioned the law of gravity and the rule of tonnage—but not much else. The undefined act of 'grumping' was disallowed, but the throwing of semi-soft or over-ripe vegetables was encouraged.

Despite all of the above, the race itself came off flawlessly. The crew of the committee boat realized that (on some strange, cosmic level) they were responsible for conducting a most bizarre sailboat race—and remembered that important fact until the end. (Amazing!!!)

At least 34 vessels officially participated. They varied from small plastic Tonka Toys to huge old three masted schooners. A good time was had by all. The weather, wind, and sea conditions were perfect. Nobody (important) drowned.

The winners felt the rating system worked well, and the losers felt it worked less well. In any event, the finishing times were fairly close. However, everyone agreed that next year, both *Silver Cloud* and *Esparanza* should be given an addition hour (or two) on their rating.

Like Tumbling Tom says, "This race, well, its S'not for everyone!"

Cruz Bay, St. John - 1990's

The Agony of Our *Triumph*

I can't believe how stupid people can be. It truly amazes me. Again and again, people whom I assume are reasonably intelligent... conclusively prove that they are not by inviting me to race with them.

They must be crazy. (I was raised by parents who kept shouting at me, "If you can't say something nice—become a journalist!" Statistically, people mentioned in my articles are 5000% more likely to commit suicide than, say, a Buddhist Monk caught child-molesting).

How could anyone who reads what I write, think, "Hey! We'll invite Fatty aboard, win the race, and he'll write wonderful stuff about us..."

Fat chance. It's never happened—and I'm beginning to think it never will.

There's something about me that seems to invite disaster. People just naturally start screwing up when I'm around. I'm sort of a magnet for ignorance, foolish risk-taking, and shoddy thinking. Beautiful things can get REAL ugly REAL quick when I'm around.

It's just something I've learned to live with. I cope as best I can—stumbling from one weird and twisted disaster to the next. Like my experience aboard the Baltic 51 *Triumph* during the 1989 Antigua Sailing Week....

The whole horrible experience actually began back in 1986—when I was being (bodily) thrown out of an expensive French restaurant on St. Barts. I was with a crazy Hungarian chick who kept taking off her clothes (nice!)—and attempting to drunkenly snatch the linen tablecloths out from under unsuspecting diner's dinners (not so nice; perhaps even rude). She kept failing, but refused to give up. ("Izzz OK," she assured me. "I used to be zeee magician's assistant, eh?... I get it thezzzzzes time, no..?")

Alas, no.

CRASH!

Heavy sigh on her part, then she'd brighten up... "OKAY/OKAY! I zinc I got it now... Vone more time, pleazzzze..!"

I would have gladly abandoned her to her fate—except she was *such* a stunner. (She made Bo Derek look like Eleanor Roosevelt.)

The cops were called—and I could hear their bicycles approaching. (St. Barts is wonderful—what other Tropical Isle features frog-pigs on wheels?) I grabbed Mz Hungary, yanked her outside, and told the restaurant owner to bill me. "Don't worry, Me-sewer Gar-song," I said in my best Frog accent. "I am a rich American Capitalist Pig—captain of the giant mega-yacht (I stupidly said the name of a large boat actually anchored out in the harbor)—and will soon send my 1st Mate ashore with some trifling amount of money for zeee damages..."

About ten minutes later—like a horrible cosmic joke—the *real* crew of the mega-yacht I'd mentioned came into the very same restaurant... and demanded a table for twenty.

They had no idea of what triggered the ensuing Gallic mini-riot, but were reported to have fought bravely against superior odds. A nice, handsome fellow named Greg was caught in the ensuing melee.

A year later in Newport, R.I. I spotted a woman strolling long-leggedly down the docks of Nigel's Newport Yachting Center. Now, Kelly was (and is) more than merely beautiful—she's the most stunning mix of race, creed, and color—the most exotic/erotic/sensuous female creature I have ever seen (or, at least, had seen *that* week). It was instant "Lust at First Sight."

I approached, and started babbling something inane about procreation, and how important it was to keep in practice. "Oh, Fatty," she smiled, "Come on back to the boat. I want you to meet my boyfriend Greg."

It didn't take us long to stumbled across the fact that I was the horrible person who had been responsible for the whole terrible mess in St. Barts. "You are soooo baaaaddd, Fatty," Kelly told me with a smile. "Isn't he, Greg?"

I swooned at her praise.

So Greg and Kelly—professional captain/crew of the pristinely maintained Baltic 51 *Triumph*—invited the entire Monkey Crew to race during the 1989 Antigua Sailing Week Regatta.

Of course, most of the Monkey Crew couldn't make it. Those not going through detox were mostly in jail. ("Betty Ford or Club Fed?") Some were on other boats; some were on other planets. Many were on a Higher Level of Consciousness—and had been since the '60's. A few had lost their name tags, and didn't remember who they were. Others were hiding out from parents, wives, children, and/or grandchildren. ("All of the above," hiccuped one old-but-hip fella.)

So I was the only Monkey Crew who flew into Antigua to join *Triumph*. It wasn't until I was actually aboard that I learned the dreaded truth.

"Our owner is aboard," said Greg and Kelly.

I looked at them with utter revulsion. "You'd better be joking," I hissed...

No such luck.

Now—as everyone who has ever played the chartering game knows—owners are a lot like fish and relatives...

...after a few days in the tropics, they begin to stink.

Of course, every rule has its exceptions—and, happily, David Muffy, owner of *Triumph*, was an *exceptional* exception.

He was an Oil Broker. I figured that anyone who spent all of their time attempting to screw both the A-rabs *and* the American People couldn't be all bad.

He wasn't. Actually, 'Murf' turned out to be an incredible guy—with a great sense of humor. He loved to laugh—even at himself—even at his own expense. During ASW '89, he got plenty of practice.

To round out the crew, we had a Real Rock Star, and a Respected Rock Pilot— plus the usual Gorgeous Gaggle of Giggling Rail Riders, Bilge Bunnies, and Racer Chasers.

The Rock Star was a Famous 12 Meter sailor whom no one had ever heard of. The Rock Pilot was a West Indian fellow who knew every rock in the Caribbean "...like de back of me hand, me son..."

I was the Token Rum Soaked Journalist—and Greg and Kelly were reduced to innocent bystanders who sat around feverishly praying we wouldn't Break the Boat Too Bad.

Their prayers were, needless to say, in vain.

The Rock Star commandeered the wheel at the start—attempting an aggressive port-tack-ahead-of-the-entire-fleet maneuver which could have worked if God was on our side... but He wasn't, so it didn't.

Dead last, dirty air—oh, well. Settle down, and sail the boat. Boat speed. Get her in the groove. Don't pinch. Power through the chop. Play the lifts. Tack on every header. Sail your own race...

The Rock Pilot posed prettily on the Aft Rail, and kept his best profile towards the Press Boat which wallowed in our wake.

I was in charge of sail trim, and kept up a steady stream of salty dialogue with nobody in particular. "Blow off the cunningham, let's have more tension on the Out Haul. Honk down on the babystay, and give me more backstay, *please*! Easy the runners. Traveler up! Ease mainsheet... there! Gimme seven pounds more halyard tension..."

Nobody actually did any of this stuff, but it made for some really neat background noise.

We were driving the boat hard, and Greg and Kelly were glancing nervously at each other as the wind and sea built. They were looking at each other like Peewee Herman might if he was practicing farting while staring into a mirror... (After all, they were going to have to fix anything and everything that went wrong...)

We were about mid-way to the first mark on the first race of the first day... my sails looked perfectly trimmed... the 12 meter guy's hair looked quite handsome... the Rock Pilot was a study in nonchalant concentration... our owner Murf was grinning ear-to-ear as we walked through our entire racing fleet to finally seize the lead...

...when we struck a submerged rock so hard I thought we'd been hit by a small nuclear weapon. The sound of our striking was awe-inspiring—my jaw dropped nearly as fast as the resale value of the boat. The shock was incredible—both physical and sticker. It snapped the radar bracket on the mainmast. ("I knew when it started raining large expensive pieces of electronics on deck that we were in serious trouble," somebody said later. Another moaned, "DooDoo occurs!")

Unfortunately, I've been on a lot of big boats hitting a lot of big things... and it's always the same weird feeling. During the first few microseconds, you shake your head and attempt to deny the Reality of the Situation. It just doesn't make sense— you can't believe that so many knowledgeable people can sail that expensive of a boat into such a large rock at such a high speed on such a sunny day...

Then you spring into action. First things first. Greg dashed below to see if we were sinking. I shouted after him, "Greg! While you're down there... bring up a couple of Cold Ones, huh?"

Priorities!

The wave which had tossed us up on the rock suddenly seemed to disappear out from underneath us... and we slid off to starboard... towards safety. I thought we were going to be okay—and then we struck the rock again. This time the stern came up, and the bow went down.

The rudder took the whole impact, and, since it was jammed hard over—it bend upwards into the counter of the vessels so hard it was hopelessly stuck.

I decided—right then and there!—to switch from beer to rum.

We sailed off the rock, but with our rudder jammed & bent hard over... we could only sail in tight circles. We tacked, and we jibed—and damn near sailed up onto the same rock again. Numerous powerboats took towlines from us, and then proceeded to hopelessly foul themselves as we spun in circles and dragged them backwards into each other. At best, it was utter chaos.

Everyone responded to the crisis in their own way. Greg allowed a single tear to leak out of his eye. Murf grabbed his side—I thought he might be getting a cramp— but then realized he was just responding to the severe economic pain which had just shot through his wallet. The 12 Meter guy took a 'solve-the-problem' approach, and began attempting to drop the rudder down far enough that we could steer. (He was hell on the gelcoat as he enthusiastically beat on the top of the rudder post with a 6 foot metal emergency tiller...) The Rock Pilot didn't say a word—he was too busy silently concocting a ridiculous series of fabrications about how he'd warned us that the rock was there... but we had all ignored him because he was (sob!) a member of an ethnic minority...

(For the record: The Helmsman asked the Pilot—approximately 45 seconds before striking the rock if he was in "good water." The Pilot stated everything was fine, there was absolutely no danger, and he'd tell the helmsman when to tack. Shortly after this reassuring statement, the Pilot was face-planted into the teak deck...)

How did I respond to the crisis? Well—keeping with my international reputation as a gentlemen—I made sure that Kelly wasn't lonely or cold or feeling neglected throughout the whole wretched ordeal...

We finally managed to get the boat to a shipyard, haul it out, and look at how well we'd 'customized' its keel and rudder.

"What should we do first," asked owner Murf.

I did *something* constructive—I made dinner reservations at one of the nicest restaurants in Antigua. We picked up Rosie, Maureen, and that strange British chick who had the anti-underwear fetish. We started out in English Harbor on *Dom Perignon*, and soon moved up to the expensive stuff. We hired a fleet of taxis to track our entourage—and 'did the island' in grand style...

...the next morning—despite being an internationally respected marine journalist on the very cutting edge of my chosen profession—I didn't know the '5 W's & the H'— the 'who, what, where, when, why, and how' of my existence.

Neither did Murf. He'd arrived in Antigua just a few days previously—the nicely dressed owner of a pristine yacht... and now he was slithering around the seediest bars of the Caribbean... clothes torn and stained... his beard wino-ragged... a crazy glint to his feverish eyes... madly in love with some Tahitian Temptress who'd washed ashore after midnight and almost drowned in our Sea of our Champagne...

"...Fatty, Fatty, Fatty," Murf was giggling as he tossed iridescent yellow/orange Cheeseballs up into the air and attempted to catch them in his mouth... "I've already made reservations at the Ad Inn for next year. Next year—if we can avoid the rocks —we'll win it! Absolutely! It's our DESTINY. For sure, or for maybe. In any event, we'll party our guts out, eh? You with me, Fatty?"

"I be your mon, Murf..." I said, marveling at what strange things people will do for fun. "I be your *mon*, mon..."

Antigua Sailing Week

An Antiguan sailor known throughout the Lesser Antilles simply as 'Yankee' sits motionless on the stern rail of the 64 foot racing sloop *Heritage* as the 40 ton vessel hurls itself directly towards the sheer cliffs of the island of Antigua. He appears to be dozing under the tropical sun. The boat—pressed hard by an enormous cloud of hi-tech Kevlar sails—is freight-training through the water at 12 knots. Touching reef or rock at such speed would surely be her death.

The 26 men in her racing crew are silent. The other vessels in the racing fleet— over a hundred of them are much further offshore in deep water. The tension on deck is thick enough to hack with a machete. Finally, helmsmen Timothy Stearns (a professional sailor, and President of Stearns Sailing Systems, Inc) glances nervously at the boat's owner Don Wildman—and speaks softly to Yankee. "Can I tack now?"

"No, Mon," says Yankee. "We be out of the current, and chasing a lift. See it up there on the water, Mon? Dancing like a cat? Steady..."

Yankee is now peering intently down—the 'lift'—a fairer wind bent by an upwind headland which allows the vessel to sail higher into the wind. *Heritage* starts pounding up the coast, sailing a shorter distance to the next racing mark than the vessels further out. Everyone on deck is grinning.

Except navigator Kevin Bosh. He's down belowdecks, hunched over his charts. He glances at his array of electronic sailing instruments—and freezes. The depth meter indicates there is less than two feet of water under the keel..!

Before Kevin can scream a warning, Yankee is shouting, "Now! NOW, Mon! Tack her NOW!!!"

The boat explodes with activity. All 26 men in the crew move with the precision of dancers. The air is filled with whistling objects Dacron ropes and stainless steel cables whip around the deck. The boom sweeps across the craft like a deadly aluminum bat. The 80 foot mast groans as it rakes the sky. The huge 'coffee grinder' winches whine as the headsail gets sheeted home on the new tack. The preventers— wire stays which prevent the mast from falling down—get released and tensioned perfectly.

Navigator Kevin Bosh is standing white-faced in the companionway as the boat gathers speed on the new tack. 'According to the depthmeter..." he says, obviously shaken, "we only had..."

"Two feet," says Yankee, grinning. "Das plenty water, Mon. Plenty water..."

Antigua Sailing Week is considered to be one of the ten best yacht races in the world—it is unquestionably the largest, most prestigious regatta in the Caribbean. This year's event was the 21st annual, and attracted 132 boats from 27 different countries. As always, it began on the last Sunday in April. As usual, the weather, wind, and sea conditions were absolutely perfect.

The regatta consists of five races 20 to 25 miles in length, with overnight stops at three different anchorages around the 108 square mile island. A massive beach party is held after each race—with colorful steel bands, reggae groups, food tents, and mobile beach bars following the fleet overland from one idyllic harbor to the next. The vessels participating in the races range in size from massive 175 foot schooners to diminutive 26 foot sloops. They race in seven different classes, for 40 different Cups.

Many of the entries sailed great distances to attend. Basil Dietholm's 41 foot Swan sloop *Sarabande V* came from Australia, Ulrich Truesse's graceful 103 foot schooner *Aschanti of Saba* came from Germany, and Colin Percy's tiny 30 sloop *Antares* is registered in Canada. Others did not sail long distances. The four French vessels from Guadeloupe only had to cruise northward for 40 ocean miles to participate.

Thirty-nine of the 132 boats were from the United States. But an almost equal number (33) came from smaller OAS (Organization of American States) nations like Antigua, Barbados, Grenada, and Trinidad. OAS nation boats (excluding the United States of America and Canada) won 17 of the 40 trophies. The Barbados boats *Blazin*, *Bruggadung* and *Morning Tide* won the prestigious Commander Nicholson Trophy for Team racing – last year it went to *Troon, Piolin & Connie D* of Venezuela. The British Virgin Island's *Stormy Weather* again captured the Mollihawk Trophy by repeating her 1986 win in the Classic Class. And *Alphida* of Bermuda took the Peter Deeth Cup for Best Performance in Cruising Class – the same cup which was won last year by *Sur* of Argentina.

As always, Argentine yacht designer Germain Frers' vessels did well. Many of his Swedish built Swan yachts were competitive this year. His *Kialoa V* – besides winning the Maxi World Championships in 1987 – has previous won first overall at Antigua twice. (Frers' designs totally dominate the 80 foot Maxi fleet. At the St. Thomas Maxi Championships in St. Thomas this year, five of the nine vessels were designed by Frers—and all three of the winners!)

The sailors themselves were as varied as their vessels. Some are fabulously wealthy. This year's winner of the coveted Lord Nelson Cup for first overall in racing class (corrected time) went to John Thomson of New York, sailing aboard his 50 foot custom Nelson/Marek sloop *Infinity*. He races to get away from the pressures of running his 50 million dollar linear bearing manufacturing company. ("Racing is something I immerse myself in to forget about business," said Thomson.) Although reluctant to discuss his fortune, he is obviously proud of the 'dinghy/support craft' which follows *Infinity* around the world to major regattas. *Affinity* is one of the finest 80 foot mega-yachts ever built—and a fine floating toy to relax aboard after a sailboat race.

Other racers have far less money. United States Virgin Island (USVI) sailor Rudy Thompson races his modest 29 foot Pearson sloop *Cold Beer* to frequent victories throughout the Caribbean. This year he won the Smirnoff Cup for fastest Class III racer in Division B. Rudy is a local legend in the Caribbean—a former charter skipper from the Good Old Days who frequently had American writer and Pulitzer Prize winner John Steinbeck aboard as a guest. "I'll never forget those days in the early 60's," says Rudy. "Steinbeck liked to steer at night—a bottle in one hand and a tiller in the other—and tell story after story after wonderful story..."

Each of these sailors come to Antigua for various reasons—to attend the world-famous beach parties, to meet the local people, or perhaps just to get away from it all. But they all have one ultimate goal—to win.

It's not easy.

Each race during Antigua Sailing Week is actually two races in one. On one level, each vessel races 'boat-for-boat' within their assigned class to see which is faster— with the first boat crossing the finish line winning 'line honors.' Bruce Fehlman's 80 foot Maxi sloop *Marlboro* from Switzerland was the fastest boat on the course this year.

More importantly, each vessel is assigned a 'rating handicap' number by the race committee which theoretically enables all vessels to compete against each other fairly on 'corrected time.' This is so vessels of various sizes and speeds can race together— and so their crews have something to argue about between races! (The crews of winning vessels almost always believe the rating system to be fair and just; the crews of losing vessels—surprise!—rarely do.)

But the rating system is all part of the fun. Antiguans are avid sailors who know they can instantly make friends with any visiting racer by merely saying, "With a fair rating, Mon, you could have WON dis ting..."

It is also a dangerous sport. At the start of the second day of racing, a 175 foot schooner from Holland crossed the entire fleet on port tack (without right-of-way), and struck three smaller vessels—poking a hole clean through one's hull. Numerous other minor collisions took place during the series, and there were three dismastings. Many boats suffered torn sails, bent spinnaker poles, and broken rigging. Miraculously, no one was seriously hurt.

Yacht racing is—at the level of Antigua Sailing Week—one of the...

no, THE most sophisticated sport in the world. To consistently win, it takes an enormous amount of talent, time, and energy by a great number of knowledgeable people. The hull designer is responsible for the boat's shape and balance. The builder must construct the boat light-in-weight, yet very strong. The rigger and the sailmaker combine their efforts to make sure the mast and the sails work perfectly together to drive the boat at its maximum speed.

All of this—and more—must be present before the first sailor steps aboard.

The larger boats in serious contention "to capture silver" usually have a 'captain' who is ultimately responsible for everything that happens, a 'driver' who steers the boat, a 'navigator' who tells the captain where the boat is and where it should go in relationship to its environment, a 'tactician' who tells the captain what the boat should do in relationship to the other racing vessels, a 'rock pilot' (like Yankee) who is intimately familiar with the local waters, a 'sail trimmer' who does just that, a 'foredeck skipper' who is responsible for having the correct sails flying correctly, and a dozen other sailors to actually carry out all the work. This isn't even mentioning the maintenance, delivery, or haul-out crews who fly in and out.

Yes, it's a sophisticated sport, and for an entire week, nearly everyone on Antigua devotes their energies to its appreciation. Most of the 80,000 year-round residents have a son, a daughter, or a husband involved in some way. It is estimated between 2,000 and 4,000 visitors arrive specifically for the competition, and pour millions of dollars directly into the economy. Local sailors, taxi drivers, and bartenders all hold strong opinions on which boat will win—and aren't shy in sharing them. Money changes hands. Reputations for shrewdness—as well as small fortunes—are made and lost. Yacht Club Commodores quiz the visiting Colorful Caribbean Characters, the ever-present Sea Gypsies, and the local boat workers in hopes of getting inside information on which boat is 'up-to-speed.' The near-by islands of Puerto Rico, The Virgins, St. Martin, St. Lucia, St. Vincent, Grenada, and the French Antilles send their finest competitors. All the United States, English, European, and Caribbean marine publications send journalists. The island is literally awash with the Beautiful People and their yachts.

Surely long-time Antiguan residents and yachtsmen Desmond Nicholson and Howard Hulford never envisioned where their simple idea of having the Antigua Hotel Association sponsor a 'little sailboat race' would lead. The Association— which had been casting about for a successful way to extend the tourist season and retain the free-spending charter yachts in English harbor for a longer period— embraced the concept wholeheartedly. The event just happened to become an international one when a Dr. Berrios of Puerto Rico

wandered by in his yacht *Enzian*, entered the race, and won! He carried
back to Puerto Rico both the Lord Nelson Cup and a glowing report of
the hospitality, warmth, and competitiveness of the Antiguan sailors.
The regatta nearly doubled in size the next year, and hasn't stopped
growing since.

"Of course," remembers Desmond Nicholson who is still the
guiding light behind the series after 21 years, "It was more laid-back
then. Not so serious. The idea was to do a little sailing—and to survive
the parties..."

Noted international yachtsman and respected marine author Donald
M. Street regularly attends Antigua Sailing Week in his 80 year old 50
foot yawl *Iolaire*. He is quick to point out the reasons he feels that
Antigua Sailing Week is growing while the USVI's Rolex Cup, and the
BVI's Spring Regatta are shrinking. "Antigua has exciting courses with
plenty of wind, sea, and scenery—and they end at different locations.
The after-race and lay-day parties are world renown. The harbor and
shoreside facilities are excellent. But perhaps the most important reason
for the growing popularity of this event is that the Antiguan people
seem interested in— first and foremost—having fun and sailing.
Hearing the sound of a cash register clacking is secondary..."

There is—indeed —something for everyone. On the two 'lay-days'
(days between races without races) there is very little laying around
done. Shoreside activities, open to everyone, abound. There are tug-a-
war games with windsurfers, sailbag races, greased pole climbing,
limbo contests, beer-drinking competitions, and wet T-shirt contests.
During the Staff of Life game, swim-suited couples have to rapidly
relay a loaf of bread between their thighs—much to the delight of the
assembled on-lookers at the Antigua Yacht Club.

One of the high points of each Antigua Sailing Week is Dockyard
Day, held the day after the last race, when the "Non-Mariners Race" is
staged. The craft—to use the term loosely—must not cost more than
$100EC ($38US) to construct, and must not have been launched prior
to the event. The result—which rapidly degenerates into a giant
demolition derby and water fight—is hysterical to watch.

Later that same evening, the Royal Antigua Police Force beats the
retreat at 1800 hours. The quaint streets of English Harbor suddenly
become deserted as everyone disappears to get dressed for the Lord
Nelson's Ball at the Admiral's Inn. This is one of THE social events of
the year; evening gowns for the ladies, and suitcoats and ties for the
gentlemen are mandatory.

The Awards are given, the politicians speak, and the competitors get
to congratulate (and commiserate with) each other. Each of the winning
yachts in their class are tied stern-to the Admiral's Inn dock where they
can be admired by all. The sounds of laughter, champagne glasses, fine

china, and sterling silver tinkle across the placid harbor.

Later that evening, formal attire in sweaty disarray, the party shifts into high gear at the Reggae bars just down the dusty road. A solid wall of electric island sound whip-saws the writhing dancers around the sandy floor. Visiting tycoons, local fishermen, and international sailors all raise a glass to the tropical heavens. The Reggae Band plays a tune written by their recently deceased Saint—Brother Bob Marley of the Wailers. "All I've ever owned are these songs of freedom," the singer croons.

The crew of *Heritage* is passing around the American Airline Gold Cup—filled with champagne which they won for being the fastest boat over 12 years old in Racing Class One, Division B. (In Racing One, Class A, they finished in second place between the 80 foot Whitbread 'Round the World' winner *Marlboro* and the locally based 72 footer *Mistress Quickly*. A very respectable showing.)

Somebody shakes a bottle of bubbly and squirts into the crowd. The tears of the vanquished are washed away by its gentle rain. Everyone is smiling.

Joel Byerley—an Englishman involved in Antigua Sailing Week from the beginning—takes a jaunt down memory lane to the early days of Antigua Sailing Week. Some of the 20 year old details have escaped from him into the mists of time. He explains: "In those days, we were too young to remember much and the future was forever..."

On the dance floor—in a checkerboard sea of black and white shining faces — a large West Indian sailor is dancing with a small elderly English woman from the BBC. He is telling her about his island's history—how the Siboney cavemen came around 4,000 B.C., the Awaraks in 35 A.D., the Caribs in 1200 A.D., the English in 1632, and the chained African slaves soon thereafter. He mentions the abolishment of slavery in 1834, the riots of 1918, and his country's total independence from England on November 1, 1981. "At last," he says with a confident, friendly smile, "The future is we!"

Racing at Antigua Sailing Week

AFTERWORD

Cap'n Fatty on *Wild Card* flying the Virgin Islands flag

Sailing into Middle Age

I am not an intellectual. I consider myself, first and foremost, a man of action. All my life I've allowed my raw emotions to rule, and have assigned my feeble brain the unenviable task of morally justifying whatever it is that my heart has done.

Why attempt to lie about it now?

I am a hedonist. I luxuriate in pleasure. I am an unabashed glutton at the table of life. Excess is the sole unifying theme of my existence.

"Just a little bit too much is just enough for me," is one of my favorite sayings. "What I lack in intelligence, I more than make up for in velocity," is another. "*You* think about it, *I'll* do it!" is, perhaps, the most basic and direct.

For over forty years I have thrived on this zestfully perverse philosophy of life.

Of course, a life dedicated to pleasure requires heavy, high-octane fuel to turbo-power it.

By three years of age I was addicted to coffee. A dozen years later, I became addicted to tobacco. And a couple of years after *that*, I 'got into' everything else. For the last 25 years I've existed on a steady diet of rot-gut rum, bloody beef, and white sugar. Whenever I felt the desire for sodium or citrus, I sucked down a bottle of tequila with all the trimmings.

But what, pray tell, has any of the above got to do with boats? This is a marine publication, isn't it?

Yes, of course it is it, Gentle Reader. And if you bear with me I'll soon get to that.

But first a quick note of rueful explanation: a writer sometimes has to be honest and truthful with his readers—no matter how much it might go against his professional grain.

It was on the second windward beat during the fifth race of the St. Thomas Yacht Club's Caribbean Laser Championship when it happened. I was tired, I'll admit. I was gulping in whole atmospheres of air just to keep going. Twice already my arms had developed cramps from the mainsheet. Half the skin on my ass had been rubbed raw by the non-skid of my Laser's deck.

I was hurting.

But I've been told repeatedly that the secret to sailing Lasers competitively is to keep 'em as flat as possible. "Flat is faster," said Peter Holmberg and Paul Dielemans and Johnny Foster, and I believed them.

So I hiked hard with gritted teeth, and attempted not to think if it was truly wise to derive some small sadistic pleasure in starboard tacking school kids less than a third of my age.

The feeling when it came was, er, arresting. Riveting. All-encompassing. It felt like someone had just clamped a large pair of electrically charged Vice Grips on my heart—and twisted. My mouth tasted coppery. My head swam.

At first, I couldn't figure out what had happened. I was underwater. My whole body had convulsed, and I'd jack-knifed myself out of the boat. Except for my feet. They were still entangled in the hiking strap. I couldn't breathe. Multicolored flashbulbs were going off behind my fluttering eyelids. I was losing strength fast.

It started to dawn on me that my situation was serious, really serious. I thought I might die.

Worse yet, I knew my boat speed had gone to hell.

"Don't panic, Fatso," I told myself. "Dis is nutt'n too serious, mon. Just get your feet free, and cling to the boat. She floats—so do we. No sweat. Easy."

It actually was easy once I'd calmed down. My feet wiggled out of the straps. I clung to the (now overturned) boat for a couple of minutes before I had enough energy to clamber back aboard and flop my butt solidly into the awash cockpit well.

I didn't sheet in or sail, just drifted off to loo'ard for about seven or eight minutes while attempting to get my breathing under control. And, of course, to assure myself that my 'muscle spasm' was over.

Finally I sheeted in slightly and hiked out gingerly—and began slowly working my way back towards the windward mark. I was 43 years old, and I'd been racing since I was eight years old. I'd never not completed any race I'd entered, and I wasn't about to start being a laggard now.

I'd finish—if it killed me.

Luckily, it didn't.

I got a DFL (Dead F'n Last), but I finished.

"How'd it go out there," asked local racer Henry Menin as I wearily pulled my battered Laser up on the beach of Cowpet Bay.

"Not too good," I admitted casually, then added, "But I think I'll be more competitive in the bar."

Silly me.

It is difficult to explain, perhaps, but the self-image of cruising sea gypsy or a competitive dinghy racer or—hell!—a normal man, for Christ's sakes...

...is based to some degree upon his physical prowess.

Of course I realize that Julian Jackson can outbox me, Holmberg outsail me, and any politician can out lie me—but those folks are professionals.

Like most men, I've always considered myself in 'pretty okay' physical shape. I might not be able to walk into any hillbilly bar in American and successfully challenge everyone within it to an arm wrestling contest—but I figured that I could wrestle with the everyday problems of life as well as the next fella. Mostly, anyway.

I've always prided myself on attitude and endurance. There have been a couple of occasions on offshore deliveries during heavy weather when I was the only person capable of standing their watch.

"Wimps!" I cackled to myself as I stood my trick (and theirs too) at the wheel. "Sissies! Momma-boys!"

And although I haven't been involved in a single act of physical violence in many years—a man's sometimes gotta convince another man that he's easier to go around than through.

Such is life, from the male perspective.

By the time I'd experienced my 'muscle spasm' three times, and twice gotten so dangerously dizzy that I nearly collapsed in public—I knew something was wrong. (Okay, so I'm not a rocket scientist!)

I thought, perhaps, I could remedy the situation by applying a tiny amount of 'moderation' to the problem. I decided to cut back to one bottle of rum a day, for instance, and have a small glass of orange juice with my three eggs, buttered grits, hash browns, toast, sliced bacon, link sausage, and country ham.

In essence, I 'went on a health kick' at least within the twisted reality of my own lush-tropical-vegetable mind.

And, since I hadn't been to one in over 20 years, I decided to see a doctor too.

The visit to the doctor started off just fine. We talked, and I took some tests. Then I took some more tests. And then I took some really serious tests.

By the time we got the last tests back, the good ole doc was breathing pretty heavily. He kept looking at the test results and then looking at me—as if my being alive didn't quite jibe with the scientific facts.

Finally, he scrambled over the top of his desk, dashed to his medicine cabinet, and started tossing plastic bottles around like a demented pill-juggler on five heavy hits of crystal meth. "Pull your shirt up, pull it up NOW!"

I barely managed to yank up my T-shirt before he rushed back in front of me, and slapped what appeared to be a large brown band-aid (Transderm-Nitro .2mg/hr) on my naked chest just over my heart. Then he collapsed in his chair once again. "There," he gasped, as he mopped his sweating brow. "That should keep you alive until you can get to the cardiologist in Puerto Rico!"

Needless to say, this bummed me out, like, BIG TIME. However, I didn't lose my common sense just because I was a bit rattled by all the gloom-and-doom talk.

I'd planned on paying him in cash. The moment he started babbling about me dying, I asked him in my sincerest tones, "Will you take a check?"

I knew the cardiologist in Puerto Rico was a true medical professional when the first thing he did was strip me of my entire life savings as I came through the door of the hospital.

Then he said: "Your heart's bad. You might not... be around much longer.... but the most important thing now is to NOT GET TOO EXCITED OR YOU MIGHT EVEN CROAK OFF SOONER!!!"

This didn't exactly put me at my ease.

Just for fun he strapped me to a dozen heart-o-meter machines, and made rueful clucking noises in the back of his throat as they all came up snake eyes. (Question: Do you know the difference between a doctor and God? Answer: God doesn't think he's a doctor!)

The worst part of my visit was the dreaded 'stress test' at the end. I almost expired before even setting foot on that miserable contraption.

In the middle of the test he shouted gaily over the roar of the galloping machine, "How are you doing?"

There I was naked, sweating, running like a demented madman while hooked to a million electrodes....

"Great," I said. "No problem. This is cool, mon, *cool!*"

I did better on the stress test than he figured I would. He seemed almost disappointed that I had not dropped dead right in mid-test. "Oh, well," his attitude seemed to be, "If you really want to prolong this process..."

I did indeed.

Thus, at the tender age of 43, I've suddenly discovered myself trapped in a horrible nightmare of clean living. I'm sober. My wife keeps careful track of my ultra strict diet. My daughter makes sure I exercise ("Mildly, daddy, mildly!") regularly as per my doctor's order.

There is a sick sort of poetic justice to this entire crazy medical situation—my being at the mercy of every vegetable I ever scorned in my entire life.

Of course I'm stoned to the gill on heart medicine. But, alas, it's not the 'tripping-the-light-fantastic' kind of stuff I (kinda) remember from the 1960's—it's more of a boring, middle-aged, migraine-headache sort of high.

Keeping to my diet is easy. I can put anything in my mouth I want. If it tastes like a mouthful of chalk and dirt sprinkled with feces—then I can safely swallow it. However, if it has any moisture or taste whatsoever, then I must spit it out. (No fat, salt or triglycerides equals no fun!)

But this whole experience has not been without its plus side: eating dust is clearly better than becoming dust.

I am still a man of the sea. I can still live aboard my vessel within the bosom of Mother Ocean. I may not be able to competitively race dinghies for a while, but I can still sail.

My life is a full one, especially in view of the alternative.

I certainly never set out to become 'mature,' but I guess a certain amount of it is forced upon you whether you want it or not. Growing old ain't for sissies.

But I've learned many lessons from the sea, and some of them apply to my current situation.

It is easy to face an offshore gale with a brand-new bullet-proof boat. But to bring a more fragile craft through a prolonged blow requires a bit more skill and knowledge. You have to ease her in the puffs, and drive her in the lulls. It can be done: it just requires a little more expertise, a more subtle touch, a steadier hand at the helm.

Life is a voyage. I still want to see what is just over the horizon. I still want to kiss life full on the lips—even if I have to have a glass of carrot juice in one hand and a hypertension sedative in the other.

Wish me luck. I'll need it. And remember not to allow me to get too far ahead of you credit-wise.

Cap'n Fatty at sea on the way to India - 2002

The Death of *Carlotta*
...an excerpt from "Chasing the Horizon"...

Carlotta is no more. I still can't believe it, though I know the above sentence is true. It doesn't seem possible. I continue to jerk awake each morning, puzzled why I'm not in my familiar bunk aboard my beloved *Carlotta*.

Then it hits me like a body-blow to the stomach. *Carlotta* is dead.

At 0623 hours on Monday September 18th, 1989, during the height of Hurricane HUGO, a 70 foot schooner named *Fly Away* dragged down on her. We were anchored in Culebra in one of the safest harbors in the Caribbean. Winds were a steady 180 knots, with gusts hitting 210 at the nearby University of Puerto Rico's meteorological station.

Fly Away literally started eating *Carlotta*. I've never experienced anything quite like it. She smashed off the port rail and whisker stays, sprung the bowsprit, and folded all the stantions. She poked holes right through the deck and bit off chunks of the cabin.

It was horrible like demented rhinos careening towards death.

For ten minutes *Fly Away* and *Carlotta* beat each other into extinction. Our exterior chainplates ripped entire planks clean out of *Fly Away*. Her bowsprit clubbed through our cockpit combings, mizzen boom, stern rail. There was nothing, absolutely nothing I could do but watch.

From midnight 'til dawn we'd told our 8 year old, life-jacketed daughter, Roma Orion, not to worry. "Don't worry, honey," my wife Carolyn would shout soothingly over the shriek of the storm. "Everything's okay. We've got four anchors down with heavy chains and long nylon rodes. *Carlotta* is strong. Look—our bunks are dry!!! We're okay. Gonna be fine. Gonna make it. Don't worry... don't worry... don't worry..."

The sounds inside *Carlotta* were more than just scary—it was enough to drive a person insane. It made you want to hold your hands over your ears... and scream too. The renting of wood. The crumbling of the concrete of our hull. The "twang" as a stay or shroud parted. The shattering of glass...

Fly Away center-punched a stantion (complete with base and life-lines) clean through our deck. It wiggled sadistically over Roma's bunk. Water poured in the boat, along with the shriek and moan of the wind.

"Can I worry now..?" asked Roma, the amazement clear in her soft little-girl voice.

By this point, *Fly Away* had dragged, inch by slow inch, astern of

Carlotta. Her bowsprit, now splintered in half, was still clubbing our battered transom.

I reached out my companionway, and grabbed *Fly Away's* only remaining anchor rode in my right hand. "Cut it! Cut it! Cut it!" my wife Carolyn screamed.

My hand went for my knife, but I stopped with it still sheathed. It didn't matter. Both our boats were doomed now. *Fly Away* had only a small anchor rode left, and she had taken out our primary 60 pound Danforth anchor, which had held us so well from midnight to dawn. It wasn't so much a matter of if we'd end up ashore—but when and how.

Just as these thoughts flew across my numbed mind—*Fly Away* snapped her only remaining anchor rode. It sounded like a cannon shot. She was gone to leeward— instant history. (I later wearily walked the shores of Culebra in a grim search and came across a floating lump of shattered lumber with the masts and rig of an old schooner piled atop. It was the broken bones and jagged flesh of the once-proud *Fly Away*.)

Amazingly, *Carlotta*, 36 feet and built solidly of ferro-cement, still held. Trees were being snatched off the mountain ahead of us, and were hitting the rig. First they'd hang up on the mainmast, then quickly work their way through the maze of stainless steel rigging wire, and then give the mizzenmast a final "whack, whack, whack" in goodbye.

I sat in the cockpit, running my 50 hp Westerbeke diesel to ease the strain on my anchors. I wore a diving mask so that I could see, and a snorkel so that I could breathe. The 200 knot gusts reminded me of some old hokey black & white movie with a fire-breathing dragon. The wind gusts were too exaggerated, too stupidly scary to be real.

A large 50 foot trawler named *Polaris* was anchored beside me. She looked so stately and safe. I glanced down at my rpm meter, and then back at Polaris. I blinked my eyes in disbelief. She was upside down. It seemed impossible—like a magic trick with mirrors. She was floating perfectly level; just completely upside down. (She never righted herself, just gradually sank with her keel and props pointed skyward...)

Carlotta kept getting knocked down by the gusts of wind. Her cockpit would fill. Once we took green water through the top of the companionway hatch. In 25,000 ocean miles, she never did anything like that.

None of this seemed possible. How could this be happening? Why were my wife and child cowering below, passports duct-taped to their soft bodies to aid some faceless Puerto Rican coroner who might later be given the sad task of ID-ing their water-logged bodies. Grim thoughts.

My life didn't flash before my eyes, but I decided that I wasn't as good a person as I should be, as moral, as kind and considerate, as caring a person as I wanted to be.

What does a man have beside his family, his friends, and his own heart?

The anchor we were now riding to (45 pound CQR with 125 feet of three-eights chain) started dragging. I literally crawled up to the bow, and veered out more scope. Nothing worked. *Carlotta's* bow fell off more, and we picked up speed. A 100 foot aluminum motorboat appeared out of the gloom. We hit it so hard on the port quarter that it rang like a bell.

A white smear—a face—appeared through a port of the motor yacht we'd struck. The face's mouth was twisted open, whether in terror or prayer or greeting or anger I could not tell.

I started laughing like a maniac through my snorkel. (I realize, now, that I was laughing in pure terror, but at the time it was almost—fun!)

I was steering my boat in 200 knots of wind to her death. We had built the boat from 12 sheets of paper 18 years ago. She had taken more than five long years and all our money to construct. *Carlotta* was more than just our boat or just our home—she was our sea-shell. She protected us in every way. Always. She was a part of us— built from our sweat, our tears, held together by our hopes and dreams and desires. She was part of the Goodlander Family.

And this, finally, was The End. Fini. Start over. Back to zero. Complete financial and emotional shipwreck.

The water all around me was frothing white. Getting into the water was death. "The water is death, the water is death, the water is death..." my brain chanted to me.

The roof of a house appeared, then a tree. The tree was in a small clearing. I steered for the clearing. We were moving fast, despite trailing three large anchors and a total of over 700 feet of anchor line and chain rode.

I felt the first sickening thud as *Carlotta* dropped her 26,000 pounds onto rock and mud and mangroves. Everything not bolted down—and a few things which were —started winging around the cabin.

We tied ourselves together with the hacked-off bitter end of a Dacron genoa sheet. We were still a family. We slid into the water, and the surf quickly swept us ashore. We were gently deposited on the manicured front lawn of a waterfront condo.

The world—at least this small portion of it—seemed totally nuts. The hurricane still screamed like the tormented souls of a million drowned sailors. The air was filled with roots, parts of boats, dinghies with 40 horse outboards, trees, sheets of tin.

We shivered and huddled together. We were dazed. Our teeth chattered in fear and excitement and maybe from the cold.

I turned and looked at *Carlotta*. She looked so lonely in her death throes. Salt water was stealing into her from holes in her hull. Fresh water was leaking in from above. Since I'd been 19 years old my life had been devoted to keeping her dry. Now I had finally failed. She was getting wet, and I was doing nothing to help her. I felt like a traitor—less than a real man.

I stood up and lurched away from Carlotta down a telephone pole/tree-barricaded road: I went in search of shelter. My wife of nearly 20 years and my 8 year old child followed.

Carlotta on Culebra - September 1989

The Last Cruise
...an excerpt from "Seadogs, Clowns and Gypsies"...

Carlotta ghosted along at dusk in the Gulfstream. The wind had gone down with the sun, and it was that quiet time between the death of the day and the rebirth of night. Carolyn, my wife and fellow sailor for the past 14 years, puttered at the galley sink. Roma Orion, our three year old daughter (who had twenty stamps in her passport on her first birthday), sat beside me in the cockpit. She waited expectantly for her nightly bedtime story.

I took a deep breath and began. "When I was a child, I lived on *Elizabeth* with my mommy and my daddy and my two sisters. And if I was good, my daddy would let me sit in the cockpit at night, and he would tell me stories about fishing and sailing and swimming. And about how the stars tell you where you are and how each ocean wave contains answers to many questions..."

"Your dad..." she said.

"Yes. My dad, your Grandpa Jim. Remember? In the hospital?"

She said nothing, but I could tell that she remembered. She had been afraid of the thin palsied hand that had reached out between the white sheets to embrace her.

Carolyn stood framed in the companionway, backlit by the soft glow of the kerosene cabin lamps. "Give your dad a hug-kiss, Roma," Carolyn said. "I'll tell you a story below. Your dad's... tired."

I steered all night, not bothering with the electric autopilot or the windvane. Sleep never entered my mind. Carolyn came up a few times and offered to take a watch, but I turned her down. I wanted to be alone with only my boat and my thoughts. I wanted to talk to my father one last time.

"Listen to the boat, son," he had told me long ago. "Ask the boat what she wants. Fools command ships, sailors guide them. A good boat is smarter than you'll ever be. The Art of Sailing is one of listening, asking, understanding. Never fight the boat; never attempt to 'beat' the sea. Accommodate them. Cooperate. Learn from them..."

His nickname was "The Guru." I remember when he earned it. During one of our annual haul-outs, *Elizabeth*, a 52 foot schooner, was next to an old yawl that had just been purchased by some college kids. A whole gang of them were working on her furiously. They were bringing her down to bare wood. It wasn't until they had her all primed and ready for the finish coats that they realized that they had ground off the boot top stripe and had no idea where the waterline went.

They came to my father for advice. "No problem," he said. "Give me the paint..."

He started at the bow on the starboard side, working his way aft. By amidships, they were concerned. "It has to be level from side to side," said one

"And straight as an arrow, or it will look awful," said another. "And, of course, it has to join up at the bow..." said a third.

My father said nothing. A commercial artist and sign painter by profession, his very eye was a straight edge. Around the other side of the boat he went, and when he reached the bow, the lines joined perfectly.

"The Guru," one of them said and jokingly fell to his knees. The name stuck. And the fact that I'd secretly helped him mark the waterline before they had ground it off didn't make him less of a "Guru" in my book, but more of one.

He loved to joke, carrying a mannequin's hand in the back pocket of his baggy shorts, tossing it to anyone working as we made our daily dock rounds, saying, "Here, let me give ya a hand..."

He wasn't famous. He never circumnavigated. He never wrote a best-selling cruising guide. But he was well liked and respected wherever cruising boats gathered in the Gulf and along the East Coast, the Mississippi River, or the Great Lakes.

Elizabeth, designed by Alden and built by Morse in 1924, wasn't in yacht-perfect shape. He preferred sailing and playing with his kids to endless maintenance.

He bought his first boat at 16 years of age. It cost more to hire a team of horses to drag it to his backyard than to purchase it. His own father said, "It will never float."

It did. And I have faded pictures of them smiling together in the cockpit as she sailed along with a bone in her teeth. My father, looking at the camera from the tiller, looked as happy as any man can be.

A few years before his death, a wonderful thing happened to him. Walking down a dock, he spotted a boat that he had owned. He hadn't seen her in over forty years. She looked better than when he had sold her.

A young man was wiping down her varnish and noticed him staring at the boat. "Hello," my father said, "I used to own her."

"I don't think so," said the young man kindly. "She has been in my family for almost 50 years. The only man that ever owned her besides us was her builder, James E. Goodlander."

"You can call me Jim," said my father. "May I come aboard?"

When Carolyn and I built our 36 foot ketch, *Carlotta*, over the course of five long, hard years, we often called him for advice. "Dad, how long should I make the chainplates?" I was 19 years old when I started.

"Have you ever sailed on a boat with chainplates that were too long or too strong..." he asked. He was like that, often answering a question with a question, allowing you to come up with your own answers. He forced you to think it through.

All of his life was spent upon the sea, learning from it, listening to it, seeking always to understand it better. When we cruised as a family in the 1950's, we were an oddity. Newspapers wrote stories about us, radio stations interviewed us, magazines sent reporters. The same question was repeated over and over. "Where are you headed next?"

And my father's answer was always the same. "See there," he'd say, pointing out to sea. "See the horizon? Well, just over the horizon, just a little further than we can see, is something so beautiful and pure, that I will spend my whole life traveling to see it..."

Once a reporter, missing the point entirely, asked, "And when do you expect to arrive?"

"Never," my father said. "I hope."

He never sailed his last boat. He was too ill to even consider it. But even so, she was his main interest in life after his family.

Near the end, he fell overboard and didn't have the strength to pull himself back aboard. For hours he hung on a dockline, yelling weakly until someone came to rescue him. Everyone thought it was terrible that his family didn't stop such a dangerous practice by such an obviously ill man. We didn't dare. And wouldn't have even if we could.

Finally, while attempting to nail some small item to a bulkhead, he realized that he didn't have the strength to lift the hammer. "Sell her," he told my mother that evening. And he never saw his beloved *Marie* again.

Growing up on the *Elizabeth* was like growing up in a fairy tale. The world was our oyster, the boat safe harbor, the family our universe. The world was a simple and just place. People were good and true and faithful. The laws of Mother Nature were fair, if unforgiving. There was a time to joke and a time to reef, a time to soak up the sun and a time to endure the frigid North wind at the helm. A very good time.

And now I am raising my own daughter aboard, attempting to give her at least a taste of the wonderful childhood with which I was blessed.

I suddenly sat upright in *Carlotta's* cockpit. Off the port bow was a misshapen orange disk—like a molten deformed dinner plate. It was dawn. Everything was perfectly still—as if the sea was holding it's breath. Waiting.

I rushed below and grabbed the urn.

His ashes were surprisingly heavy. Multi-colored and textured. I said some words —words too private to repeat in print. I poured him into the deep blue waters of the Gulf Stream to voyage endlessly and eternally. I set him free on his last cruise.

And as I poured his ashes into the sea, for an instant the world shifted and I saw the future. And it was not my hand pouring my father, but my child's hand pouring me into the ocean. I was over-come with a feeling of wholeness and goodness such as I had never experienced before.

As I watched the ashes disappear astern, a gentle wind heeled *Carlotta*. She started chuckling along, heading for the Lesser Antilles a thousand miles away.

The world was still a true and just place. Mother Nature was still fair, if unforgiving. People were still good.

And I was blessed with a fine sailing breeze.

"Good-bye, Dad," I whispered into the wind.

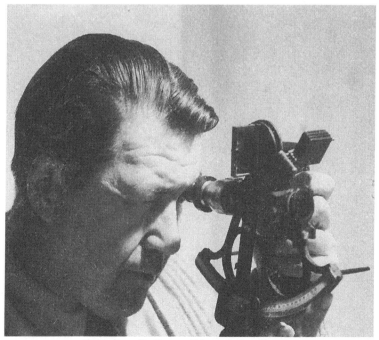

"The Guru" - James Edward Goodlander

Also available from **Cap'n Fatty Goodlander**:

Seadogs, Clowns, & Gypsies is more than just a book about the remarkable lifestyle of various Caribbean sailors. It is a Celebration of a Way of Life. The people who inhabit these salt-stained pages ("We're all here, because we're not all there!") have a true Lust for Living. They kiss life full on the lips, embrace each new day, welcome every fresh sensation.

Yeah, they are louts and cads and drunkards and misfits and fools – and yet, somehow, they emerge from these yarns as a noble, vital people.

————————

Chasing the Horizon is a delightfully demented Celebration of A Way of Life. It is an outrageously funny, often touching, and continuously shocking tale of a modern sea gypsy.

Cap'n Fatty's story is too bizarre to be fiction. Father wears floral skirts; mother is a tad vague. Sister Carole isn't interested in her millionaire suitor; she's too busy smooching with the kid in the cesspool truck. Their strange live-aboard boat caravan includes Mort the Mortician, Backwards Bernie, Ruby Red the Conman, Barefoot Benny, Geeper Creeper, Para the Paranoid, Lusty Laura, Xlax, Shark Boy, the Pawtucket Pirate, Bait Broad, Colonel Crispy, Scupper Lips, Bob the Broker, the Pirate Queen, Otto the Owner, the Twin Slaves of Green Slime—and even a terribly long-winded fellow named (Hurricane) Hugo. All seem hell-bent on avoiding the cops, the creeps, each other, and especially the Dreaded Dream Crushers.

Dive in!

Order direct from Amazon.com
(also available in Kindle editions)
or order through our website at:
fattygoodlander.com

Cap'n Fatty Goodlander has lived aboard various
sailing craft for 48 of his 56 years. He is editor-at-large for Cruising
World magazine and is currently producing a series of Southeast Asia
travel spots for National Public Radio.

He lives aboard his 38 foot sloop *Wild Card* with his wife Carolyn, and
at the time of this publication, is heading across the Indian Ocean
toward Africa.

4197082

Made in the USA
Charleston, SC
11 December 2009